Daniel W. Cathell

The Physician Himself and What He Should Add to His Scientific Acquirements

Fourth Edition

Daniel W. Cathell

The Physician Himself and What He Should Add to His Scientific Acquirements
Fourth Edition

ISBN/EAN: 9783337869670

Printed in Europe, USA, Canada, Australia, Japan

Cover: Foto ©Andreas Hilbeck / pixelio.de

More available books at **www.hansebooks.com**

THE PHYSICIAN HIMSELF

AND

WHAT HE SHOULD ADD

TO

HIS SCIENTIFIC ACQUIREMENTS

IN ORDER TO SECURE SUCCESS.

BY

D. W. CATHELL, M. D.

LATE PROFESSOR OF PATHOLOGY IN THE COLLEGE OF PHYSICIANS AND SURGEONS OF BALTIMORE.

FOURTH EDITION.

ENLARGED BY THE ADDITION OF NEARLY THREE HUNDRED NEW
SUGGESTIONS.

BALTIMORE:
CUSHINGS & BAILEY,
226 W. BALTIMORE ST.
1885.

PRESS OF ISAAC FRIEDENWALD,
BALTIMORE, MD.

THIS LITTLE WORK

IS RESPECTFULLY DEDICATED TO

PROFESSOR AUSTIN FLINT, Senior,

IN ADMIRATION

OF HIS VARIOUS CONTRIBUTIONS

TO SCIENTIFIC MEDICINE,

AND OF HIS

UNTIRING DEVOTION TO THE WELFARE

OF OUR PROFESSION.

PREFACE TO THE FOURTH EDITION.

ASSURANCES have been received from every quarter, that the publication of this little work was timely, and that it is materially assisting in the advancement of the interests of our profession, and the welfare of its members.

This is highly gratifying to the author, and repays him a thousandfold for the labor of writing it.

In preparing a fourth edition, he has carefully revised the entire work, and made such alterations in existing paragraphs, as greater experience and more mature reflection have dictated, and has added a great many new suggestions, which he confidently believes make this of much greater value than the former editions.

PREFACE TO THE FIRST EDITION.

OBSERVATION has impressed the author with the belief that an essay on PERSONAL QUESTIONS IN MEDICAL PRACTICE, would be of decided benefit to numerous members of the profession. He has therefore, with diffidence, attempted the duty and jotted down the following thoughts as they suggested themselves to him in the course of a busy life, and now publishes them in the hope that they may awaken a proper degree of attention to this class of subjects in the minds of his professional brethren.

The entire work has been written in the form of a reply to a question, for the purpose of making what is said appear more direct and personal to the reader.

D. W. C.

2 N. BROADWAY, BALTIMORE.

THE PHYSICIAN HIMSELF

AND

What he should add to his Scientific Acquirements in order to secure Success.

CHAPTER I.

"Things small in themselves, have often a far-reaching significance."—Chew.

A certain amount of professional tact and business sagacity is as necessary to the physician as the mariner's compass is to the navigator. There are gentlemen in the ranks of our profession who are perfectly acquainted with the scientific aspects of medicine, and can tell you what to do for almost every ailment that afflicts humanity, who, nevertheless, after earnest trial, have never achieved either reputation or practice, because they lack *professional tact and business sagacity;* and there is nothing more pitiful than to see a worthy physician deficient in these qualities, waiting year after year for a practice, and a consequent sphere of professional usefulness, that never come.

Were a young physician to ask me: What honorable means can I employ, in addition to scientific knowledge and book-learning, in order to make my success in practice more certain, more rapid, and more complete? I should offer him the following suggestions :

You should, above all else, strive to start right, and to enter promptly on the road to success; for unless you make some mark, acquire a reputation and build up a practice in your first six or eight years, the probabilities are that you never will.

It is better not to enter into partnership with other physicians. Partners are usually not equally matched in industry, tact and similar qualities, and are not equally liked by the public. Hence the union generally does not prove as beneficial or as satisfactory as expected, and consequently partnerships rarely continue long. Above all else, never ally yourself with any other doctor except as an equal. Julius Cæsar said, "I had rather be the first man in a village than the second man in a great city."

The location and appearance of your office will have a great deal to do with your progress. Select one in a genteel neighborhood, upon, or very near, an artery of travel, convenient to either a densely populated old section, or a rapidly growing new one. If you were to locate on a back, or unfrequented street, or other out-of-the way place, it would naturally suggest to the public either defective ambition, or distrust of your own acquirements.

Remember, in making your selection, that a doctor cannot rely on his near neighbors for patronage; people in his immediate neighborhood may never employ him, while some farther away will have no one else.

Branch offices are as a rule not desirable. Besides consuming valuable time in going to and fro, and in general occasioning double trouble, they create an uncertainty in the minds of those seeking the doctor, as to where he may most readily be found. On estimating all the advantages and disadvantages, therefore, I think it will be found that a plurality of offices increases greatly neither one's practice, one's popularity, nor one's income, and may be regarded as likely to prove more annoying than profitable.

It is risky for a beginner to locate too near a group of popular, energetic physicians, as their superior advantages and established reputations may keep him dwarfed for too long a time.

If possible, have a good, light, airy and accessible office, one that is not used for a family parlor, or any other accessory purpose.

Exercise care in its arrangement; let it look fresh, neat and clean, thus showing that its occupant is possessed of taste and gentility, as well as learning and skill; and at the same time that it is not a lawyer's consulting-room, nor a clergyman's sanctum, nor a smoker's parlor, but the office of an earnest, working, scientific physician, who has a library, takes the journals, and uses the various instruments science has devised for him.

Take care, however, to avoid running into a quackish display of the latter, and keep from sight such inappropriate or even repulsive objects, as catheters, specula, obstetric forceps, splints, trusses, amputating knives, skeletons, jars of amputated extremities, tumors, and the unripe fruit of the uterus.

It is not unprofessional, however, to allow to be exposed your microscope, stethoscope and other aids to precision in diagnosis, diplomas, certificates of society membership, pictures of eminent professional friends and teachers, anatomical plates, professional relics and keepsakes, or anything else that is specially associated with your medical studies and career. But it is better to limit such articles to those having relation to you as a student or physician.

A case of medicines, cabinet of minerals, or works of art, are in good taste; so also are your dictionaries, encyclopedias and lexicons for ready reference; but let no sharks' heads, impaled butterflies, bugs, miniature ships, snakes, stuffed birds, lizards, hornets' nests, or anything else be seen that will place you in any other light than that of a physician. If you have a love for such things, at least keep them out of sight of the public, and endeavor to lead every observer to think of you only as a physician.

Display no political or religious emblems, portraits, etc., about your office, because these relate to your personal sentiments, and your office is a public place, not for any special class, but for every kind of people; no matter what shade of partisan or sectarian pictures you may display, they will surely be repugnant to some.

Establish a regular professional and business policy at the beginning of your career. Have your office lighted punctually every evening, at the proper hour, and in all other respects let it show attention and system.

Do not allow the ladies of the family to lounge about your office, read your books, answer the office bell, etc., lest it repel patients. Both messengers and patients would rather meet the doctor, or his servant, than ladies. You should respect public opinion in this and in all other matters justly open to criticism.

A physician is judged by the company he keeps. Avoid associating with those who bear a merited stigma, or are notoriously deficient, or whose hopes and ambitions have been blighted by their own misconduct. Let your associations be, as far as possible, with professional brethren and people of genuine worth. Prefer to spend your idle time in your office, or at the drug stores, or with other doctors, or at the medical library, to lounging around club rooms, cigar stores, billiard parlors, barber shops, etc. No ordinary man ever conceives a more exalted opinion of a professional man by fraternizing with him at such places.

Be cordial with all kinds of patients, but do not handshake and harmonize unreservedly; undue familiarity shears many juniors of much of their prestige. Never become so familiar as to lay all formality aside and enter any patient's house, or room, without ringing, knocking, or calling.

Never have companionship with Irregulars; it would detract from both you and rational medicine, which you represent, and give countenance to delusions and pretenders; avoid this, and every other contaminating alliance.

What shall be said of debauchery with harlots and association with concubines? Of drinking and of gambling? My dear sir, if you have entered any one of these roads, turn from it at once, for they all lead downward, and will destroy your finer sensibilities, prove fatal to every ambition, and finally blast your career. Now if any one of these habits singly will be attended by such fatal consequences, what must be the combined effects of them all? Professional suicide! Virtue alone will make you happy and enable you to withstand your critics.

Put not a feather's weight upon the honorable ambition of any one, or a straw in the pathway of his worthy aspirations, but be very cautious how you involve yourself by inducing young men to study medicine, as there are already three doctors where one is required. Besides, either their misconduct or unfair rivalry may work injury to yourself.

It is not usually either profitable or advisable to take office students, as they are necessarily in your way and divert your mind from other duties; but if you should do so, charge them for the privilege not less than the usual fee of $100, each, per annum. And only take such applicants as have a reputable character, good sense, mental and physical vigor, the necessary educational qualifications, and honorable ambition. Refuse all such as are prompted to embrace medicine from a belief that its study is simply a pleasant pastime, or that it is less laborious than the business they have been following, or who are tempted by the ease with which a diploma can be obtained, or by a false idea that it is a smooth and royal road to moneymaking, or by any other motive so unworthy.

Do not let your office be a lounging place, or a smoking room for horsejockeys, dog-fanciers, gamesters, swaggerers, politicians, coxcombs, beaux, sports and others, whose time hangs heavily on their hands. The public look upon physicians as serious, sober men, who have been singled out and set apart for a lofty purpose, and as worthy of an esteem not accorded to such people, or to persons engaged in the ordinary business of life. The conversation and amusements of such company do not harmonize with the tastes and desires of physicians of refinement, and, moreover, they tend to weaken or destroy the faith of the public, which is so essential in our work; on no profession does faith have such influence as on ours. The public takes cognizance of these and of a great many other little things regarding medical men; in fact, every circumstance in your manner, appearance, conversation, habits, etc., will be closely observed and criticized, more especially in the early years of your career.

In getting office signs, remember that a doctor has them, not as advertisements, but simply to show his office to those looking for him. Your signs should be neither too large nor too numerous. One of black smalt with gold letters is the neatest and most attractive of all; one such sign on the front wall for the daytime, and a glass one with black letters in the window, to be seen at night, when your office is lighted, are sufficient. The letters on the former should be round and well shaped, and not more than two inches high, with corresponding width.

All signs should be neatly made and properly lettered, for even a sign makes an impression, either good or bad, on the public, and first impressions are very enduring.

It is better to put Dr. . . . . ., on your sign, than to put . . . , M. D. "Doctor" looks better and is understood by all.

To put "Physician and Surgeon" or "Physician and

Accoucheur," or other compound title on your sign, would be superfluous, since all physicians are surgeons. As well might the confectioner say on his sign, " Cold Ice Cream."

Unless there is danger of your being confounded with some other doctor of the same name, it is well to omit your given name, or initials, from your signs, but it should be on your cards. Of course, if your name is " Smith," or " Jones," or " Brown," it would be neces- sary to put your given name on your signs; but if your name is uncommon, it is not. People would not speak of Doctor John W. Garfield, but of Doctor Garfield.

Do not allow other people's signs of tooth-drawing, cupping and leeching, millinery, dressmaking, painting and glazing, boarding, etc., in company with yours.

It is unprofessional to put where you graduated and how long you have practised, upon your cards and signs, or in the newspapers.

Establish regular office hours early in your career, and post them conspicuously in your office ; also have them on your cards.

It may be a question whether it is advantageous to have a sign designating your office hours on your office window, or on the outside front, to show them to the out- side public. Your situation in business should influence your decision on this point. A young physician, or one who has much spare time at home, in addition to his stated hours, would be more apt to catch the over- flow, emergencies, cases of accident, or calls from strangers in the city, and other anxious seekers for " any one, so he is a doctor," and who have perhaps searched and found all the busier physicians away from their offices. These calls you would be likely to get, if an exhibition of your office hours does not drive them off by showing them before ringing the bell that they have come at the wrong time, when in fact you are at home and ready for calls. On the contrary, one busily engaged in outside practice, who has no other time for office consultations than the specified hours, can, by displaying them outside, regulate matters better, and prevent various annoyances, by letting every one see his hours before ringing.

An excellent rule is to direct attention to both the beginning and ending of your office hours, as : " Morning office hours begin at 7 and end at 9. Afternoon office hours begin," etc., etc. Many people think that as your office hours are from 7 to 9, if they get there one minute before 9 o'clock they are in time; whereas if they come at that time they will be sure to keep you past your hour for going out. By regulating your time thus, and constantly urging those you attend to observe those hours strictly, you can accomplish doubly as much with less hurry and more satisfaction to all. Indeed, by persistently schooling patients to observe those hours, and send for you, as far as possible, before your accustomed time for starting on your regular rounds, you will do much to systematize your business, and to lessen the number of calls at odd and inconvenient times, which do so much to increase the hardships of the Doctor's life.

If you should ever get very busy, and be pressed for time, your sign might still further emphasize it, after stating your hours, by adding, " No office consultation at other hours."

Have on a little sign over your slate something like this: "In leaving a message for the Doctor, be careful to write the name, street and number."

You should keep a supply of cards with your name, residence, and office hours on them. An inch and three-quarters by three inches makes a good size. It is also necessary to keep a supply of small and neat blank bills, and to have envelopes and paper with your name and address printed on them. Let your bills read "For professional services." Blank forms for use in giving certificates to sick members of societies, etc., are also very useful. Printed professional certificates look much better, seem more formal, and give more satisfaction than written ones.

A speaking-tube from your outside office door to your bedroom is of the greatest utility for night calls.

The telephone is also both a luxury and a necessity. Many physicians who need a telephone are deterred from getting it by the fear that it will cause them to be summoned to patients, good and bad, at a distance too great for them to attend, or that its convenience will cause annoying calls and messages to be received at unseasonable hours. This belief is erroneous. The telephone really does the opposite, and cuts off the long arguments and attempts to over-persuade that we encounter in personal interviews. It is much easier to refuse a call, or to make a plea, or give a direction, or order a remedy, through the telephone, than by an interview with a messenger.

When you begin practice, get a pocket visiting-list, a cash book and a ledger, and commence to keep regular accounts at once; this will teach you system, and in the course of time save you hundreds of dollars.

Record the full name, occupation, and residence of every new patient; for, although the identity of this one and that one may, at present, be very clear in your mind, yet as patients multiply and years elapse, your recollection of various ones will become misty and confused, and the consequent loss to you will be very great.

Never neglect to make memoranda of office consultations, payments, new calls, etc., in your visiting list, with a lead pencil, until you get an opportunity to write them in ink.

Have a copy of the fee-table framed and hung in a conspicuous position in your office, that you may refer patients to it, whenever occasion requires. Also, have a small, neat sign, with "Office Consultations from $1 to $10," posted in some semi-prominent place in your office. It will show your rule and tell your charge; it will also remind those who really forget to pay, of the fact, and will put less honest people in a dilemma. You can, when necessary, point to it and ask for your fee, and let them know you keep no books for office patients. Such a sign will save you many a misunderstanding and many a dollar. Of course you may omit its cash enforcement towards persons with whom you have a regular account.

Having your charge from "$1 to $10," will enable you to get an extra fee for cases of an extraordinary character, and still allow you to charge minimum fees for ordinary cases. Such a schedule will make those who get off by paying the lowest fees, feel gratified; it will also show everybody that you are skilful enough to attend ten-dollar cases.

Cultivate office practice assiduously; for it is a fertile source of reputation and of cash fees. Try to benefit and give satisfaction to every patient that comes to consult you, that every one may go away with a clear idea of what is the matter with him, and a belief that you will do your best to remedy it; for each will, while there, form some definite opinion in regard to you, and will ever after give you either a good or a bad name.

Keep a small case of medicines for use at your office, representing the most frequently employed articles of the pharmacopœia, especially during the first years of practice; handling them will not only familiarize you with their appearance, odor, miscibility, taste, and other characteristics, but also enable you to get fees from patients who can appreciate advice and medicine combined, but who cannot appreciate advice alone. Besides, by keeping cathartic pills, aromatic spirits of ammonia, lime water, morphia granules, etc., you can, by sending a suitable remedy by a messenger, save yourself many a tramp at night, during storms, on Sundays, great holidays, at odd hours, etc., and yet give the patient both relief and satisfaction, till you can go.

You have a perfect right to supply a patient with medicine, if you choose. Very extensive use of this privilege, however, tends to consume valuable time, to dwarf you in other ways, and does not pay. Besides, it would engender the criticism and enmity of neighboring druggists.

When you are summoned to cases of colic, convulsions,

accident, etc., go, if possible, immediately. Then, if you are too late, you will have no cause for regret, and neither be chagrined, nor responsible. When you cannot go at once, without neglecting other duties equally as urgent, it is much more satisfactory to your patient, if you send a remedy with instructions for use till you can go, than to send a prescription; to send a prescription in such cases seems rather as if you do not care to attend, or as if the patient was on your secondary list, and if the case does not eventuate favorably, you may be severely criticized.

If, at your office and elsewhere, you make an honest and proper use of instruments of precision—the stethoscope, ophthalmoscope, laryngoscope, the clinical thermometer and microscope, and those used in making urinary analyses, etc., they will not only assist you very materially in diagnosis, but will also aid you greatly in curing people by heightening their confidence in you and enlisting their co-operation.

Always carry in your pocket case a good clinical thermometer, a female catheter, a bistoury, a hypodermic syringe, a pair of small forceps, a stick of lunar caustic, a penknife, etc., for ready use. Keep a little raw cotton in the case with your clinical thermometer, to protect it against breakage, and always wash the instrument immediately after use.

Avoid syphilitic inoculation, septicæmia, etc., in making vaginal and other examinations. Cosmoline and vaseline answer very well; they have no affinity for moisture, and both keep for years without becoming rancid or decomposing. Get a pound can of either, and keep it in your office for anointing your fingers, instruments, etc. Wooden toothpicks and wooden cigar-lighters are very handy for making mops, applying caustics, etc. Being inexpensive, they can be thrown away after one service, instead of being kept for further use, as must be done with expensive articles.

Knives, probes, needles, etc., can be readily cleaned and disinfected, both before and after being used, by thrusting them several times through a cake of wet soap.

Be careful never to immerse a finger that is even abraded, in vaginal or other suspicious fluids; if your preferable hand is unsafe, use the other.

You should have a special receptacle in your office for cast-off dressings from cases of gonorrhœa, syphilis, septic ulcers, etc., which, when they accumulate, should be burned.

You should live comfortably for the sake of being comfortable, and rest as much as possible on Sundays and at *night; and if you would avoid the risk of breaking down your physical health, as hundreds of our profession do, consider it a cardinal duty to get your meals and your sleep as regularly as possible.

Every physician should keep himself neat and tidy, and should avoid slovenliness and everything approaching to carelessness or neglect; above all else, he should wear a scrupulously clean shirt and a spotless collar. You never heard of a bank swindler, or a confidence-man, or a gambler, or a counterfeiter, or pseudo gentleman of any kind, who dressed shabbily or appeared coarse. Such people are all close students of human nature, and no matter how abandoned they are, no matter how tarnished their characters, nor how blackened their hearts, they manage to hide their deformities as with a veil from all but the few that know their true characters, by assuming the dress and manners of gentlemen. Now if genteel dress and polished manners can do so much for such fallen specimens of mankind, how much greater influence must they exert for those who are truly gentlemen and members of an honorable profession.

Do not ignore the fashions of the day. A due regard to the customs prevailing around you will show your good sense and discretion. Even though the prevailing style of dress or living border on the absurd or extravagant, it may still be wise to conform to it to a certain extent. Young says:

> "Though wrong the mode, comply; more sense is shewn
> In wearing others' follies than our own."

Do not, however, be a leader in frivolous fashions, appearing as though your foppishness had overshadowed everything else ; nor display glaring neckties, flashy breastpins, fancy canes or any other peculiarity that indicates a desire to be a society man or a swell. Such individuals may be admired, but they are not usually chosen by worthy persons seeking a guardian for their health.

Even though you are ever so poor, let it be genteel poverty, for a physician's dress, manners and bearing should all agree with his dignified calling. The neglect of neatness of dress and the want of polite, refined manners might cause you to be criticized and shunned. You will see some whose heads are comparatively empty succeed almost entirely by attention to appearances and affability of manner, while many much better qualified will fail by reason of defects in these apparently trivial matters. Clean hands, well-shaved face, polished boots, neat cuffs, gloves, fashionable clothing, cane, sun umbrella, all indicate gentility and self-respect, and give one a pleasurable consciousness of being well dressed and presentable.

The majority of people will employ a well-dressed physician more readily than a shabbily dressed one; they will also accord to him more confidence, and expect from and pay to him larger bills.

Avoid double callings. Divorce medicine from everything else—from the drug business, from giving public readings, from singings, poetry, concerts, base-ball playing, rowing matches, etc., because the public cannot appreciate you or any one else, in two dissimilar characters, half doctor and half druggist, or three-eighths doctor and five-eighths politician, or other similar mixture of incongruities, for it is in medicine as in religion—no one can serve two masters. Although it may seem paradoxical, even reputation as a surgeon (though surgery is but a branch of our art), or as a specialist of any kind, militates decidedly against reputation in other departments of medicine. The public in general believe a surgeon is good only for cutting, and that a specialist is good only for his specialty.

Hesitate even to take such offices as vaccine physician, coroner, city dispensary physician, sanitary inspector, etc., in a section where you expect to practice in future. All such functions seem to dwarf one's ultimate progress, and usually create a low-grade reputation that it is hard to outlive. To many people, all such offices look somewhat like a confession of impecuniosity, or inferiority, and create an impression that is not overcome for years. If you have any merit at all, private practice industriously followed will lead by better roads to speedier success.

The last remark is, also, to a certain extent true of the position of physician or assistant physician to hospitals, asylums, dispensaries, etc., where the employment at a nominal salary and the comforts of a home, for a few years, have caused many a physician fully qualified for success, to lose the best part of his life, and let slip opportunities that could never be recalled.

Politics, even when honorably pursued, are ruinous to a young physician's prospects; later, when his medical reputation is already extensive, they will militate against him, although they may not necessarily ruin him. If honorable politics injure thus, how much worse is it to be drawn into low ward demagogism and wirepulling at primary meetings. You can in the long run make ten friends and ten dollars by medicine while you are making one of either by politics, beside escaping many anxious hours and bitter disappointments.

You will also find that society, church, political and other special groups of patients, gained because they are affiliated with you in party matters, rather than through appreciation of your merits as a physician, are neither very profitable nor very constant. Banishing every thing that comes between you and your legitimate work, and cultivating patients secured promiscuously from every direction, because they have faith in your skill as a physician, will in the long run pay you better than attending to politics or any other outside issue.

A riding physician has several advantages over the one who walks; he gets rest while riding from one patient to another, and can spend the time in thinking; can collect and concentrate his mind more fully on his cases while riding than if walking, and when he reaches his patient he is in proper mental and physical condition to begin his duties, while the walking physician arrives tired and in need of rest. Another convenience is, he can salute acquaintances as his carriage meets them and ride on, whereas were he on foot he might be compelled to stop, parley and lose valuable time with convalescent patients, old friends, etc.

You should, therefore, get a respectable-looking horse and carriage, as soon as circumstances will at all justify. A team is not only a source of health and enjoyment, in the beginning of practice, but getting it indicates that your practice is growing. Many persons consider success the chief test of merit, and prefer a much-employed physician. This is one of the reasons why any one can RIDE into a full business much quicker than he can walk into one. Besides, the inexperienced public, with nothing else to judge by, infer that a physician who rides must have had extensive experience and a successful practice, else he would not require and could not afford it.

If you unfortunately have a bony horse and a seedy-looking or unsuitable kind of carriage, do not let them stand in front of your office for hours at a time, as if to advertise your poverty, lack of taste, or paucity of practice.

If you have two horses, it is better to drive singly, that one may be resting while the other is working. Driven thus, two good, well-kept horses can carry you to as many patients as you can attend.

It is perfectly fair and proper to seek reputation by all legitimate means, but careful observation will convince you that attempts to attract attention by quack devices, driving ostentatious double teams, or having liveried drivers, odd-shaped or odd-colored vehicles, close carriages, conspicuous running-gear, or blazed-faced, curious-looking horses, or ponies, or by habitually driving as though the devil were in chase, and attempting to read a book as the carriage whirls and jolts along, also affecting odd-style or extra wide brim hats, long hair, heavy canes, etc., all generally fail in their object, are looked upon by many as the efforts of a small mind or weak head to hide a lack of ordinary skill, and actually bring the one who affects them into ridicule and disrespect. Do not thus belittle yourself, but strictly avoid ostentation and every peculiarity of manner, dress, office arrangement, etc., calculated to excite either ridicule or contempt. On the other hand, however, if you are shame-faced, diffident, lacking in aggressiveness, or deficient in tact, you will never prosper, until these disadvantages are overcome.

It is customary and proper to give notice of removals, recovery from long sickness, return from long journeys, etc., in the newspapers, but it is not creditable to announce your entrance into practice, or to advertise yourself generally in newspapers, or to placard barber shops, hotels, etc. Puffing yourself, your cases, your apparatus, or your skill, or winking at being puffed and applauded in the papers, is quackish, and on a par with the speckled-horse plan. A proper pursuit of medicine will imbue you with loftier sentiments and engender nobler efforts to gain public attention, and will spur you to build your fame on stronger foundations.

Cultivate a professional manner and spirit. Do nothing to gain popular favor that does not accord with both the letter and the spirit of the code. Independent of the degradation you would feel, it would not pay to trust for business to tricks of any kind ; for the veil that covers such attempts is generally too thin to hide the real motive, or to turn aside ridicule.

You will be more esteemed by patients who call at your office for any purpose, if they find you engaged in your professional duties and studies, than if reading novels, making toy steamboats, or occupied in other non-professional pursuits; even reading the newspapers, smoking, etc., at times proper for study and business, have an ill effect on public opinion. Public opinion is the creator, the source of all reputation, whether good or bad, and should be respected; for a good reputation is a large, a very large part of a physician's capital.

It is very natural to expect your medical neighbors to pay you a friendly visit after you locate, whether acquainted or not; but if they fail to do so, it should not be construed as ill-will, for it may be due to their position of doubt concerning your being regular, etc., which they for the time being entertain. Very true men are sometimes slow to fraternize.

There is a very great difference between the case of

an additional physician starting in a community or neighborhood, and an additional person being added in almost any other business. The demand for other things can be increased, but the demand for doctors is limited, so that a new doctor must create his practice out of that taken from other physicians. Every family the newcomer adds to his list must be diverted from that of a rival, who may have attended it long enough to almost deem it his private property, and of course the rival does not like it; for there is a little human nature still left in a man, even though he has studied medicine. The older practitioners are therefore naturally very apt to be watchful of, if not captious towards their new rival, and when they see him crowding himself in, much as we see one do in an already crowded street-car, animosities and feuds are apt to arise. There is a proverbial rancor about medical antagonisms and medical hatreds; avoid them as far as lies in your power. Courteous rivalry between doctors is advantageous to the public, because it creates a spirit of emulation, and compels each to try to be skilful and successful in practice.

It is in fact almost natural for an established physician to regret the advent of another medical aspirant; and some are sensitive and hypercritical towards every newcomer to a degree bordering on monomania, because the stranger, in coming, must exert a perturbing effect on the professional business of those already established. His coming makes more workers, and if he is skilful, actually makes less sickness; because the spur of rivalry stimulates each to try to get all curable cases well, not only surely, but quickly. Sickness, both in amount and duration, is decreased, because skilled laborers have increased. There is, of course, no greater number of cracked skulls, dislocated bones, sore legs, cases of rheumatism, or diseases of any kind, than before the stranger came. He must therefore draw his share of the loaves and fishes from the others.

Study the manœuvres of that ungrateful bird the cuckoo; how the fostered cuckoo expels all the other birds from their maternal nest after its cunning mother has been unwisely allowed to deposit an egg, and their parent has watched and nourished it, until it is strong enough to show its ingratitude by hurling the rightful owners out, and you will realize why established doctors dislike to see interlopers gain a foothold in their section, and effect an entrance into their families. Competitive practice does not necessitate enmity; but self-preservation is the first law of nature, and when it is endangered, every human bosom feels the same impulse.

If you are conscious of any merit above mediocrity, if you are ahead of your brethren, let mere matters of display remain secondary, while your merit is made the more prominent. This is more durable, less expensive, and more in harmony with the views of sensible people. Do not hesitate, however, to embrace every accidental or natural advantage in practice, if honest and ethical.

You will find that intellect, genius, temperance, correct personal habits, and other excellent qualities, will all fail unless you add ambition, self-reliance and aggressiveness to them; but in your efforts to advance, you should take care not to incur the reputation of being a sharper, or of being tricky. If the balance were struck, it would probably be found a great deal harder for a physician to worm and intrigue his way through life, than to struggle along with honesty and industry. Determine, therefore, that in your efforts you will do nothing that is criminal, nothing that will not stand every test and the severest scrutiny, nothing for which you would hesitate to sue for your fee, if necessary—nothing that you cannot approve of, with your hand on your heart and your face turned upwards.

CHAPTER II.

There has been of late years a disproportionate annual addition to our already overcrowded profession, and the colleges of the United States—with only an exceptional, and that a very rudimentary preliminary examination into literary qualifications, and with inducements, such as small fees, short terms, condensed lectures, coaching and cramming, and the brief two years' course required for obtaining a degree—are sending out annually more than 2000 physicians, and this does not include those who reach our shores from abroad, already prepared to enter upon practice. The result is, that there are now in every community, probably, three or four doctors where one is really needed. Canada has one for every 1193 inhabitants, Austria one for every 2500, Germany one for every 3000, Great Britain one for every 1652, France one for every 1814; while we of the United States, blessed in physicians as in everything else, have, counting both regulars and irregulars, one for every 600; and druggists in proportion. If there were only twice as many as needed, it might be wholesome, and would allow the public a choice, but, with such an excess as this, many worthy ones must necessarily languish, and those who flourish must do so by great skill, great tact or great industry.

[32]

The medical door—and the window, too—is open, wide open, to every variety of individual, and all kinds have entered; and you will be unusually lucky if you encounter none who are maliciously antagonistic. You will not only meet Dr. Willing, Dr. Fair and Dr. Bland, but Dr. Cynic, Dr. Oblique, Dr. Sneerer, Dr. Crusty, Dr. Broiler and Dr. Frigid are also about and may be sometimes encountered. Let your conduct be fair and square to every such person on all occasions. And strive to build a reputation for uprightness that will excite the respect of all whether friendly or inimical to you, and convince them that you are incapable of any dishonorable act.

Never begin making reprisals, nor enter into a wordy war with a rival; avoid all innuendoes and sarcastic remarks to the laity about opponents who have offended you. Resolve that you will remain a gentleman, even under provocation, whether others do or not. Observe the Golden Rule with dignity, " Do unto others as you would have them do unto you," and trust the balance to time. Medicine is an honorable calling; resolve that it shall be no less so by your embracing it. Remember that honor and duty require you to do right, not for policy's sake, but because it is right. Do not, however, expect exact justice from enemies in return ; for were you as chaste as ice, as pure as the snow that falls from heaven, you could not escape misrepresentation by adversaries with evil eyes and lying tongues.

Although you cannot stop people's tongues, nor their evil talk about you, yet you must see that nothing is allowed to blast your reputation for honorable conduct. Charges against your skill, unless very gross and dam--

3

aging, had better be left unnoticed; even though it reaches your ears that some person has said he has a total lack of faith in you, and would not call you to attend a sick kitten, etc., etc., such talk need not disturb your equanimity—remember that such remarks are not personal, but simply expressions of lack of faith in you professionally. Such things are said about every physician in the world, and although they grate harshly when they reach the ear of the one they concern, they are quite different from personal libels—such as charges of being a drunkard, or an adulterer, or an abortionist.

Be circumspect in boasting of the number of cases you have, of your wonderful cures, or of the surprisingly large amount of your collections. All such things are apt to create envy, disbelief, criticism and other hurtful results. Also avoid telling from house to house how busy you are, and of your numerous bad cases—as if to swell your own importance. Indeed, it is better to be silent in regard to your own merits and to relate nothing at all to laymen about any case but the one before you; to do so will not enhance you any, and if you really have extra cases and extra skill, people will be sure to find it out in other ways. Also avoid the habit of talking to people about your collections, bills, etc., unless it is to a person about his own bill, or you will soon get the reputation of thinking and talking more about money matters than anything else.

As a physician, you will require a good address and a variety of talents, for you must come in contact with all kinds of people. Readiness in adapting yourself to all classes sufficiently for the requirements of your profession, is a very useful quality, and one in which most physicians are very deficient.

In addition to medical learning, you should strive to possess an acquaintance with general scientific subjects which exercise the reason, rather than the memory, and also look into general literature, that you may be on a conversational level with the best you meet, and sustain the reputation for liberal and polite learning, and love of wisdom, naturally accorded to all physicians by the public.

A good preliminary education, although not indispensably necessary to the acquirement of skill, experience and success as a physician, is a powerful element of success in the professional struggle; and if·yours is defective, the deficiency should be made up by honest study as fully as possible; otherwise it will debar you from ever obtaining more than a limited elevation in the profession. Without a fair education, you will be continually exposed to ridicule by your use of bad grammar or spelling, from those who are, perhaps, your inferiors in skill and common sense. But I doubt the wisdom of frittering away, after practice is begun, a disproportionate amount of precious time on light literature, educational frivolities, and schoolboy subjects, or giving them at all more than recreative attention allows. Nor is it wise to give special attention to higher mathematics, the fine arts, agriculture, mineralogy, botany, geology, or other collateral studies, while yet imperfect in the practical branches of medicine proper; because simultaneous attention to a plurality of subjects would prevent concentration of thoughts, and naturally divide and distract your mind, and prevent you from pursuing the more important with your full strength. But whatever studies you do undertake, should be pressed with determination and system till accomplished.

The plan of forcing themselves to tenaciously pursue certain aims of a practical character, constitutes the peculiarity of most practitioners who succeed in an eminent degree. This is not only true in medicine, but in any calling. I once knew a person who by accident lost his leg at the middle of the thigh; previous to this he was but an ordinary swimmer, but afterwards, the fact of his having only one leg attracted great attention to his swimming. Seeing himself thus observed, stimulated him always to do his best, which made him more and more expert, until eventually he became the best swimmer I ever saw, because the most ambitious.

If you have not had the advantages of embracing Latin in your early education, you should not fail to employ a good Latin scholar to teach you, at least as much as you need in your practice; you can get one at a nominal cost by advertising anonymously in any daily paper. He can, with the aid of a grammar and a dictionary, teach you in a short time, sufficient of this language to enable you to write prescriptions, etc., correctly, and thereby lift you above a feeling of deficiency in this important particular. Besides, ability to write your prescriptions in correct Latin naturally assists in creating respect, or rather, in preventing unfriendly criticism and disrespect for you in the minds of your fellow-physicians, the druggists, and others.

Many people actually believe we write prescriptions

in Latin to conceal the ingredients. The true intent is, of course, to give every article a concise and specific title, and point it out in such a manner that when it is prescribed, it may be known from all others, and mistakes of meaning between the prescriber and the compounder be prevented; besides, the Latin names of drugs are the same in America, Europe and elsewhere, and can be read by the scholars of every nation, while the common name is liable to differ with each nation and locality. Latin is a dead language, belonging to no modern nation, and therefore not subject to mutations. It is not only accurate, but has become highly respectable by long usage.

A rudimentary knowledge of Greek is also quite useful, as from it have been formed most of the compound terms employed in the medical and other sciences.

In using Latin names of medicines, and of diseases, muscles, etc., be consistent. Adopt either the English or the continental pronunciation, but whichever you adopt, be careful to use it invariably, and correctly. Try to acquire a correct pronunciation of medical terms by frequently consulting a dictionary, of which there is none better than Dunglison's latest edition.

An acquaintance with the German language is not only pleasurable and a means of intellectual improvement that costs but little money, but it will assist you greatly with the Germans, among whom you will find many of your most honest and grateful patients. Determine to get at least a smattering of German early in your career.

You will find that many foreigners prefer an American

physician who can speak their language, to one who has come here from their own country; because, being a native, they know he has spent his whole lifetime here, and they reason that he is naturally more familiar with the diseases that exist in our climate, and with the modifying influences of our seasons, diet, etc.

Accustom yourself to use current and correct orthography, to write in a good, neat, distinct and legible hand. Write every prescription as though critics were to judge you by it; each ingredient on a separate line, principal ingredients on the first, adjunct on the next, and vehicle on the last, unless you have some special reason for inverting them. Such a system insures well-balanced prescriptions, disciplines the prescriber, and engenders the respect and favorable criticism of all who notice it.

Strictly avoid incompatibles, both chemical and physiological, such as the combination of chlorate of potassium with tannic acid or with sulphur, oxide of silver with creasote, etc., which are explosives and may blow up either the dispenser or the patient. Charcoal is a simple thing—sulphur is another simple thing, and saltpetre is still another, but put them together and you have gunpowder, which is not simple, and unless that potent agent is intended, look out. Remember, however, that some medicines, though physiologically incompatible, are not therapeutically so, as under certain circumstances you may combine them so that they may modify each other, as morphia and belladonna, acetate of lead and sulphate of zinc, etc. It is better to use a single remedy, or, if two are indicated, to alternate them, unless you know they are compatible. The list of incompatibles is a long one, but you should learn it by heart, rather than take any risk.

Try to make every prescription you write show on its face, that you intend it to meet some specific indication.

Be careful that abbreviations of names, manner of writing quantities, etc., leave no room for mistake. A good rule is, to read carefully every prescription after you finish writing it.

You, of course, need not be told that while the names of the various ingredients in a prescription should be written in Latin, the directions, i. e. all that follows the S. (Signa), should be in English, as they are intended for the guidance of the patient.

It is a bad habit to adopt a routine in prescribing and slavishly to follow your own, or anybody else's, stereotyped formulæ for certain diseases. Suit your remedies to the case, instead of picking out a ready-made formula from your collection for the patient, as you would a hat in a hat store. One formula for all diarrhœas, for instance, is about as apt to suit every case of loose bowels, as one coat is to fit every man in a regiment.

Remember that skill in practice consists not only in diagnosis, prognosis, and prescribing medicine, but is the combined result of all the powers that the physician legitimately brings into the management of cases. In other words, the skilful use of medicine is but *one* of many elements that make the unit of medical skill. You must study mankind as well as medicine, and remember when working on diseased bodies that they are inhabited by minds that have warm sentiments, strong passions and vivid imaginations, which sway them powerfully both in health and in disease. To be successful you should fathom each patient's mind, discover its peculiarities, and conduct your efforts in harmony with its conditions. Let hope, expectation, faith, contentment, fear, resolution, will, and other psychological aids be your constant levers, for they may each at times exercise legitimate power. It is not length of time in practice, but study and reflection that teach the use of these. If you are not a keen observer of men and things, if you cannot read the book of human nature correctly, and unite knowledge of physic with an understanding of the thoughts, feeling and desires of mankind, with the knowledge of the effects of love, fear, grief, anger, malice, envy, lust, and other strong but hidden passions that govern our race, you will be sadly deficient, even after twenty years' experience.

Your professional fame is your chief capital; ambition to increase it by all legitimate means is not only fair, but commendable. After you attain it, you will not be apt to lose either it or the practice it ensures, so long as you are sober, decent and discreet in conduct, and have the physical health to endure your labors.

A pure, virtuous mind is a great gift and a great aid to success. When elopements, seductions, confinements, or abortions, or the scandal about Dr. —— or Rev. ——, or Miss ——, or the ignobleness of the pedigree of this one, or the secret history of that one, are being talked of, you should have a silent, or at least a prudent tongue; all you say on such subjects will surely be magnified and retailed, and its result will be a permanent injury to you. The position of the gossiping physician has ever been a very bad one, and he is not unfrequently called to unpleasant account.

Remember, while in contact with scandalmongers, to take care, and, if possible, keep the conversation on general or abstract subjects, instead of descanting upon individuals and private affairs.

Notice the never-failing advantage that refined people with pure minds and delicate language have in every station of life over the coarse and the vulgar, and in view thereof let your manner, conversation, jokes, etc., be always chaste and pure. Never forget yourself in this particular, for nothing is so hurtful to a physician as the exhibition of an impure mind. School yourself to avoid every impropriety of manner, and never allow yourself to become insensible to the demands of modesty and virtue. Chasten every thought, purify every word, and measure every phase of your deportment, if you would succeed fully, especially if gynæcology and obstetrics are part of your ambition. A lewd-minded physician who indulges in coarse ambiguities, vulgar jokes and indelicate anecdotes about the sexes, is sure to be shunned, and the reason therefor is sure to be made the subject of gossip, and passed from one to another till it reaches the purest and best of the community. Thinkers of both sexes everywhere regard such physicians (and rightfully so) as being far worse than those who drink, cheat and swear.

When duty requires you to ask questions on delicate topics, or to broach very private subjects, do so with a manner of gravity and simplicity, not too direct on the one hand, nor with too much circumlocution on the other.

If your manners and conversation are of the kind that win and conciliate rather than repel children, it will be fortunate, and will put many a dollar into your pocket that might have gone to some homœopath. Fondling, kissing and dallying with people's children, however, are liable to be misconstrued into an effort to secure the good will of the parents for selfish motives, and should be avoided.

A cold, cheerless, passive manner toward patients, isolation of oneself from them socially, and failure to recognize would-be friends on the streets and elsewhere, as if from a lofty independence, destroy all warmth towards a physician, and usually cause their possessor to fail to inspire either friendly likings or faith ; and no physician who cannot in some way make friends or awaken confidence in himself, can succeed. The reputation of being a " very nice man " is even more potent with many than skill. To be affable and skilful too makes a very strong combination—one that is apt to waft its possessor up to the top wave of popularity. If one is especially polished in manner and moderately well versed in medicine, his politeness will do him a great deal more good with the public than the most profound acquaintance with histology, microscopic pathology and other scientific acquirements.

Cheerfulness is a never-failing source of influence. Medicine, contrary to the general belief, is not a gloomy, morose profession, but a bright, cheerful one. While allaying pain, curing some poor wretches and relieving others in body and administering hope and comfort to their minds, you will fully realize the great good your profession enables you to do, and will naturally feel happy and satisfied with yourself and with your life-work, and this should make your cheerfulness apparent.

Study to acquire an agreeable and professional manner of approaching the sick, and taking leave of them. There is an art in entering the patient's room with a calm, earnest manner that shows interest and an anxiety to learn his condition—making the necessary examination, ordering the remedies, and then departing with a cheerful, self-satisfied demeanor that inspires confidence on the part of the patient and his friends, and a belief that you can and will do for him all that the science of medicine teaches any one to do. The appearance, the walk, the movements, the language, the gestures and mode of intercourse of some physicians are pleasing; of others, rude, harsh and repulsive to the sick.

Familiarity with the many little details of the sick-room—including the art of making beef teas, gruels, poultices, &c., and with the minor operations you are there incidentally called on to perform, create a very favorable impression. Indeed, it is to a very great extent by these that watchful nurses and other habitues of the sick-room judge you.

The art of keeping hope and confidence alive in the bosom of the patient and of his friends is a great one ; a bright, fresh countenance and an easy, cheerful, soothing manner is a power that will nearly always infuse tranquility and repose into your patient's mind and carry him with you towards recovery. A cheering word sometimes does as much good as a prescription.

It is very pleasing to the sick to be allowed to tell in their own way whatever they deem it important for you to know ; allow every one a fair hearing, and even though they are tedious, do not abruptly cut them short, but listen with respectful attention. A patient may deem a symptom very important that you know to be otherwise, yet he will not be satisfied with your views unless you show sufficient interest in all the symptoms to at least hear them described. Where, for want of time to listen further or where the recital becomes too irrelevant, check him not by a rude order " to stop," but by asking him to show his tongue; this has often served my purpose with garrulous women and others.

To be quick to see and understand your duty, and equally prompt and resolute in doing it, as if possessed of inborn acuteness of perception, and of intuitive skill, is one of the strongest points you can possess. People invariably applaud boldness ; indeed, a bold, prompt act, if successful, often leads almost to idolatry.

Flexibility of manner, self-command, quick discernment, address, ready knowledge of human nature and ability to adapt yourself to the ever-changing phases of medical practice, are great necessities.

We meet patients of various and even of directly opposite temperaments and qualities; the refined lady, and the hodcarrier, the beer-seller and the clergyman, the aged and the young, the hopeful and the despondent, the diffident and the bold, the deep and the superficial. Let every one find in you his ideal. Seek to penetrate the character of each, and to become perfect in the power of adjusting your manner and language to the case before you.

If you have the ability to control your temper, and to maintain a cool philosophic composure under the thousand provocations given to physicians, it will give you great advantage over those who cannot, and it will generally redound greatly to your credit.

A brusque, autocratic manner is bad for a physician unless sustained by unquestionable skill, or reputation. A gentle, urbane, but firm manner is suitable to the largest part of the community. Remember that a stiff, unfeeling, abrupt or arbitrary manner, is quite different from the philosophic composure acquired by constant attendance on the sick and suffering. The former is brutal and unprofessional, the latter is essential to enable you to weigh correctly and manage diseases skilfully.

If you have any genuine idiosyncrasy it will be noticed, and, if not disagreeable, will aid you greatly: but never assume one, as the counterfeit is easily detected by all sensible men and women. Act out your own plain natural character everywhere and at all times. Besides being ridiculous, a physician who assumes a fictitious or borrowed manner, must be either wrong-hearted or weak-headed.

If you have the gift of fluency in conversation, or sweetness of manner, or great native courtesy, or a never-failing stock of politeness, or a knack for illustrating your points by apt comparisons, or a bold way of unravelling the various puzzles, or cutting the many Gordian knots so often encountered, it will help you decidedly. If, on the contrary, there is any necessary aid that you lack, study and practise constantly to acquire it.

Ability to communicate your opinion of a case to the inquiring friends of the patient, in well chosen, proper and satisfying language, is a quality so useful that you must endeavor to acquire it.

Act toward children and nervous patients so as to remove all dread of your visits ; avoid a solemn and formal, or funereal manner, as it would give rise to dread of you, especially if you accompany it with a corresponding mode of dress. If your air and movements are naturally awkward, or sombre, set them off by cheerfulness, suitable dress, etc.

When you visit a patient, neither tarry long enough to become a bore and compel the wish that you would go, nor make your visit so brief or abrupt as to leave the patient feeling that you have not given his case the necessary attention.

Showing an earnest, anxious, gentle interest in the welfare of patients, as if you were present in mind, as well as body, is another very strong faith-inspiring quality. To assure a sufferer that you will take the same care of him as though he were your "own brother," or in case it be a female, as if she were your "own sister," or will attend a child as if it were "one of your own family," or to assure a woman in labor, that you will be as gentle in making the necessary examinations as if she were an infant, and similar truthfully-meant expressions of sincere sympathy and interest, inspire wonderful confidence, and are often quoted long after the physician has used them.

The world is full of objects of pity. Probably no busy physician can give full time and exert his entire

skill in every case that appeals to him, or throw into it
his whole heart, undivided thoughts and intellectual
strength, or even feel deep personal absorption in the
sufferings of every patient to whom he is called ; if he
did, the endless chain of misery he sees would, through
over-care and grief, soon unfit him for active practice.
But you can, and should, at least, manifest some anxiety
and interest in all cases, and avoid exhibiting indifference
in any. Approach the sick with soft steps, and use
kind words with them. The possession of humanity,
or the lack of it, in a physician, can in no way be so
accurately judged, as when he is questioning and examining the sick — the soothing voice, the cautious
touch, etc., all do a great deal to soften the pillow of
sorrow and affliction.

Be very careful to avoid inflicting pain in examining
the sick, and assuage their fears and over-sensitiveness
by assurances that you will not cause any more suffering than is unavoidable, and then make your words true.
Whoever has any such manner, naturally will not, can not
fail to get devoted patients, who will willingly trust and
retain him in preference to all others, even though they
know his general reputation for skill to be far below
mediocrity.

You must depend for success chiefly, of course, on
your skill in curing the sick. You will find nevertheless that but few patients, probably not one in twenty,
can judge the amount of technical and scientific knowledge you possess. The majority are governed by
the care and the devotion you exhibit, and form their
opinion of you and measure your services by the little

details of routine attention, which is another evidence that the scientific is not all that is necessary.

Be especially courteous and civil to lady attendants of the sick. Woman is, and ever will be, the angel of the sickroom; and you as a physician will see many touching illustrations of her tender ministrations and heroic devotion as mother, wife, sister or friend to the sick and suffering, even to the sacrifice of her own life.

After a patient convalesces, or when it is not necessary to attend him daily, if, when you are in his neighborhood, you send to inquire how he is getting along, it will not only give you the desired information, but will also impress everybody with a grateful sense of your interest in the case.

Having a sick child taken up for examination, carrying your patient to the light that you may see him fully and examine him carefully, having his urine, or his sputa, or the blood he spits, etc., saved for examination, will not only give you very necessary information as to the patient's condition, but also satisfy him and everybody else of your interest and solicitude, and of your anxiety to do your whole duty. So also does paying one the first visit in the morning and the last at night, or staying, in urgent cases, to see that the medicine produces the desired effect.

You will find that in times of sudden sickness and alarm in families, there is a peculiar susceptibility to strong impressions. Kindness shown then is doubly appreciated. Indifference or coldness, on the contrary, may then sever attachments and end friendships that have existed between the physician and a family for years, in as many moments. Many a young physician secures a good family permanently by kindness and assiduous attention in cases of colic, convulsions and accident; or by faithful, devoted and unwearied attention in cases of typhoid fever, scarlet fever, etc.

A potent lever to assist in establishing your professional reputation lies in curing the long-standing cases so often seen among the poverty-stricken. Many of these poor disease-ridden creatures are curable, but require greater attention to the details, and a great deal more care and personal superintendence than older physicians whose time is monopolized by acute cases, can possibly devote to them. If you persevere with them until a cure is effected, your special interest will be observed and appreciated, and you will gain a host of warm admirers, who will magnify and herald you forth on every occasion as being doubly skilful in making the blind see, the deaf hear, and the lame to walk, and even though you receive little, or no reward from them in the shape of money, you will augment your fame, and cultivate both your hand and your eye, and school yourself in the art of observing, analyzing and treating disease.

You will find it comparatively easy to get practice among the moneyless poor, and relatively hard to get it among the wealthier classes. Your reputation will probably begin in alleys and back streets, among the very poorest, where it will extend much more rapidly than in comfortable quarters; but no matter whether in mansion, cottage or hovel, every patient you attend, white or black, rich or poor, will aid in enriching your

4

experience and shaping public opinion by giving you either a good or a bad name.

Attending the servants of the rich, however, who are sick at their service places, will not improve your reputation much ; at any rate, not nearly so much as attending the same patients at their own homes, or on their own account. People who, in their minds, couple you professionally with their servants, are apt to form a low opinion of your status and of the character of your practice.

Nor will you find it very satisfactory to attend people who "just call you in to see a sick member of their family" *because* you are attending across the street or in the neighborhood. Those who select you, or send for you because they prefer you to all others, will be your best patients.

You are not obliged to assume charge of any one, or to engage to attend a woman in confinement, or to involve yourself in any way against your wish ; but, after doing so, you are morally and legally bound to attend, and to attend properly, even though it may be a charity or "never pay" patient. You have a right, however, to withdraw from any case by giving proper notice.

Remember that ethical duties and legal restraints are as binding in pauper and charity cases as in any other, for ethics and law both rest upon abstract principles, and govern all cases alike.

You will probably find hospital and dispensary patients, soldiers, sailors, and the poor, much easier to attend than the higher classes ; their ailments are more definite and uncomplicated, the therapeutics more clearly indicated, and the response of their system is generally more prompt. With the wealthy and pampered, on the other hand, there is often such a concatenation of unrelated or chronic symptoms, or they are described in such indefinite or exaggerated phrases, that it is difficult to judge which one symptom is most important.

With hospital patients, sailors, soldiers, etc., there are but two classes—the really sick, suffering from affections of a well-marked type, and malingerers. Such practice is apt to lead to a rough and ready habit of treating every patient as very sick, or else as having little or nothing the matter with him. These crude or possibly over-active methods may answer in public institutions, but they will not suit the squeamish people with indefinite or frivolous ailments, for which the physician trained only in a hospital could hardly fail to feel and manifest contempt. Hospital practice is so different from private that but few members of our profession shine conspicuously as practitioners in both spheres. An illustration of this fact is constantly afforded in the colleges and in medical societies ; for the greatest medical orators and the most fluent debaters are by no means always the best or most successful practitioners. The two fields are essentially different and lead the mind in different directions. In a word, theory is one thing, practice another.

It is your duty to familiarize yourself at the very threshold of your professional career with the Code of Ethics, and never to violate either its letter or its spirit, but always scrupulously to observe both towards all *regular* graduates practising as *regular* physicians. But remember that you are neither required nor allowed to extend its favoring provisions to any one practising *contrary to* the cherished truths that guide the regular profession, no matter who or what he may be.

I am not sure that the medical profession of any other country besides ours has a code of written ethics. Possibly old countries from long custom can dispense with them. But here the very nature of society requires that physicians shall have some general system of written ethics, to define their duties and regulate their conduct towards each other and the public. Every individual in the profession is supposed to be a gentleman, actuated by a lofty professional spirit, striving to do right and avoid wrong, and even were there no written rules at all, the vast majority would naturally conform to the rules of justice, at least as they understood them. As a consequence, each one's action, when scanned by watchful and knowing eyes, might probably be considered fair in nine doubtful cases out of ten, while in the tenth, one might conclude differently from one's neighbor, or might be found differing in opinion only from some captious rival with whom an honorable agreement would be impossible. The absence of rules for our government would also leave each individual to make his own code, and no matter how crooked his ways, no one could charge that he acted from impure motives and not from error of judgment, even in the most flagrant violation of humanity's Golden Rule.

Absence of a code would also make it possible for the unscrupulous to carry on a regular system of infringements, self-advertising, certificate-giving, and wrong-doing in general, regardless of the rights of their professional brethren, and still claim to be honorable physicians, whilst those aggrieved would have no standard of appeal by which to prove the contrary.

In view of these and many other facts it has been found necessary to have a code of written ethics for regulating the conduct of physicians towards each other, and towards the public generally.

Dr. Thomas Percival, an English physician, in a small book published in London in 1807, proposed an admirable code of ethics, which, excepting a few alterations made necessary by the lapse of time and the advance of medical science, is the identical code adopted by the American Medical Association in 1847, and which from then until now has governed our whole profession throughout this broad land, just as the Ten Commandments of Holy Writ instruct and restrict mankind in general.

The author, in common with almost the entire profession, regrets to see that a factious minority of the physicians of New York, becoming restive under the wise provisions of the code forbidding professional consultations with homœopaths, and other kindred exclusionists and followers of isms, have abjured the code, and proved themselves ingenious architects of ruin to themselves, as their action has severed them from their brethren, without securing for them the fellowship of those Ishmaelites whom they wished to conciliate. May this be the fate of all rebels against what is right and just!

All physicians are supposed to have studied this code, and to be familiar with its requirements. The claim which it has upon you rests not upon any obligation of personal friendship toward your professional brethren, but upon the fact that it is founded on the broad basis of equal rights and equal privileges to every member of the profession, that it stands like a lighthouse to guide and direct all who wish to pursue an honorable course. Being founded on the highest moral principles, its precepts can never become useless, till regenerate and infallible human nature makes both codes and commandments unnecessary. The code of ethics of the American Medical Association is the great oracle to which you can resort, in order to learn what things justice allows and what it prohibits.

To these lofty ethics, in very great measure, are due the binding together and elevation far above ordinary avocations of the medical profession of our land, and the esteem and honorable standing which it everywhere enjoys.

By its dignity and justness this code remains as fresh and beautiful to-day as when the profession adopted it nearly forty years ago, and if you faithfully observe it, you can truthfully exclaim, "I feel within me a peace above all earthly dignities, a clear and quiet conscience."

It is as much the duty of every medical college in America to acquaint its students with the precepts of this code and to furnish to each of its alumni a copy of it with his diploma, as for a mother to familiarize her children with the Ten Commandments.

In our land this code is the balance-wheel that regulates all professional action, and no one, either among the eminent of the profession, covered with honors and titles, or among beginners in the ranks, can openly ignore it without overthrowing that which is vital to his standing among medical men. If in the struggle and competition for business you desire to act unfairly toward your brethren, this code will compel you to do the evil biddings of your heart in a roundabout way, or by stealth, and even then your unfairness will seldom go undetected or unpunished. The great God of Heaven has declared that "whatsoever a man soweth, that shall he also reap." Any one upon whom you encroach in an unprofessional manner will feel himself justified in retaliating with your own weapons, and you will reap a crop similar to the seed sown. Whenever you sow a thistle or a thorn you will reap thistles or thorns, whenever a wind is sown a whirlwind will be reaped; whilst the sweeter seeds sown by others will be yielding to others sweeter fruits.

When called to attend a case previously under the care of another physician, especially if the patient and friends are dissatisfied with the treatment, or if the case is likely to prove fatal, do not disparage the previous attendant by expressing a wish that you had been called sooner, or criticize his conduct or his remedies; it is cowardly and mean to do either. Remember in all such cases to reply to the questions of the patient or his inquiring friends, that your duty is *with the present and future, not with the past.* Refuse either to examine or criticize the previous attendant's remedies. Also, make your conversation refer strictly to the present and future and not to the past, and do not mention the person you have superseded at all, unless you can speak clearly to his advantage. As a rule, the less you say about the previous treatment the better.

To take a mean advantage of any one you have super‑ seded, besides being wrong, might engender a profes‑ sional hornet, which in retaliation would watch with a malignant eye and sting fiercely wherever opportunity offered. Avoid finesse. Courtesy, truth and justice should mark every step of your career. Enhance your profession in public esteem at every opportunity, and defend your brethren, and your profession too, when either are unjustly assailed. Indeed, to fail to defend the reputation of an absent professional brother, when justice demands it, is ignoble and unprofessional, and implies a quasi-sanction of the libel.

We all know there are a thousand unwritten ways to be ethical, and a thousand undefinable ways to be un‑ ethical. When you doubt whether a patient is fairly yours or another's, give your rival the benefit of that doubt. Never be tenacious of doubtful rights, but let your conduct in this, and all other respects, entitle you to the esteem of your medical neighbors.

Do not captiously follow up every trifling infringe‑ ment, difficulty, or apparent contradiction; a certain amount of jarring and clashing in a profession like ours is unavoidable. Allow liberally for this, school your feelings, bury captiousness in the ocean of oblivion, and maintain your friendly attitude toward all fairly dis‑ posed neighbors. Unless you do this, many questions will arise that cannot be adjusted by the code, and you will become involved in useless, rancorous and endless controversies and reprisals. It is both embarrassing and inconvenient to pass and repass medical neighbors between whom and yourself there exists a chronic feud, or to meet any one else with whom, through enmity, friendship and even speaking acquaintance have ceased.

Keep above all doubtful expedients that relate to getting patients and profits, and be careful not to run into any other physician's practice, and never attempt unjustly to retain any one to whom you are called in an emergency ; if you are in doubt whether you were deliberately chosen, or only taken in the emergency, ask the direct question. If another was preferred to you, surrender the patient to him on his arrival, even though you are asked to continue in attendance. Circumstances may require you to have the former attendant sent for, either to take the case, or for consultation.

Friendly offices are daily performed by physicians for one another, and go far, very far, toward neutralizing the ruffles and stings which the very nature of our profession makes inevitable. If your conduct towards other physicians in these matters is invariably honorable and just, arising from a desire to do only that which is right, it will be discovered in due time, and will make your road pleasant, and if you ever unwittingly infringe, all will feel that it is through mistake and not intentional.

Never visit a patient who is under the care of another physician, as a medical detective for the patient's beneficial society, to ascertain whether he is malingering, without that physician's consent. It would be a still greater offence to remove the bandages from fractures, ulcers, etc., put on by another physician, whether to change treatment or merely to examine the case.

Be also extremely discreet and chary of visiting

patients under the care of other physicians, even for social purposes, as it is a frequent cause of suspicion and contention.

Never take charge of a patient recently under the care of any other regular physician, without first ascertaining that he has been formally notified of the change. The idea that governs such cases is this : When a person sickens he is at liberty to select any physician he prefers, but after making a selection, and when the case has been taken charge of, if for any reason whatever he wants to change, he must follow the established form in doing so. If there are any hard thoughts against the other physician, or unpleasant scenes with him, the patient and his friends should have them, not you.

The dissatisfied persons who wish to dismiss their attendant and get you, will sometimes contend that the rules regulating the taking charge of patients, recently under the care of another physician, are harsh and unjust and peculiar to the medical profession. Neither of these statements is true, as our custom is identical with that which prevails everywhere among all classes of people the world over, and which requires the formal discharge of the old employe, before a new one can take his place. Besides, no person, whether laborer, mechanic or physician, can fill a vacancy till one exists.

You should never suggest that an attending physician be discharged, so that you may be employed.

Be chary of taking cases in families into which you have ever been called in consultation, more especially if you were called at the other physician's suggestion, for the displaced attendant, chagrined at his displacement, will be apt to scan every feature of the change, and if he has any ground at all, will conclude that instead of obeying the Golden Rule, you have ungenerously elbowed him out.

You will often be called to a patient, and upon going, will find that he is under the care of some other physician, and will, of course, refuse to attend, but you will almost surely be urged just to look at the patient and tell what you think, or to prescribe for him, with the promise that the other physician shall not be told of your having done it. Remember that honor and duty require you to do right in these and all other positions in which you may be placed, and that not through fear, or for policy sake, but because it is right to do right, and for the other equally broad reason that you yourself would know of the wrong, whether the other physician knew it or not; decline, therefore, their solicitations, with an assurance that you desire to possess your own respect, as earnestly as you do that of others. Unless a great emergency exists, you should positively refuse to interfere; if you do consent, it should be done for the attending physician, and you should leave a note telling him what you have done. Take care to make no charges for such services.

When persons are inveighing to you against an attending physician, and finding fault with his treatment, you should never suggest that he be discharged, so that you may supplant him.

The rules regarding previous attendance are much less stringent in floating office practice than in regular family practice, and some of the most eminent physicians prescribe for all ordinary office cases, with but little regard as to who has been attending, or where, or when. A patient with heart trouble, cough, or a skin disease, will occasionally consult almost a dozen physicians at their offices in as many days. The principle is this: Office advice to strangers is everywhere cash, and the payment of the fee frees the patient to go to whomsoever else he pleases.

You will see much to condemn in regard to ethics, both in the profession and in the laity. If you are ever compelled to attack any one's conduct, do it boldly, or at least never do it anonymously or in whispers; anonymous and covert attacks are cowardly.

Be punctilious in your endeavors to do every one justice. If you err at all in this respect, let it be in liberality. Suffer injustice, rather than participate in it. Sometimes, even though the letter of ethics allows you to take a patient, it may be unkind, or unwise to do so; use such opportunities to harmonize, rather than to disrupt. You can do this, and yet not make a habit of cheating yourself out of patients.

Always keep a stock of good vaccine on hand, both for the fees it secures, when there is a demand for vaccination, and for fear of a sudden outbreak of small-pox.

Vaccination, although a trifling operation, is a prolific cause of criticism and reproach to physicians. Use calf virus whenever it is possible to obtain it; it is popular, and not capable of communicating syphilis, scrofula, etc., and needs no defence. In no case use any but pure virus; take your time and do it skilfully and thoroughly, and be ever ready to defend its purity with proof, if any one you vaccinate suffers any mishap through it.

Do not begin the unjust custom of vaccinating the child GRATIS, in cases where you have officiated at its birth, as is the habit with some. Also charge the same for revaccinating any one to test whether his former vaccination is still protective or not, as you would if he never had been vaccinated before, whether it takes or not, as revaccination succeeds in but a small proportion of those it is tried upon, and the charge is for the trial.

You should, of course, make no extra charge for repeating primary vaccinations till they take, no matter how long the interval between the trials ; also, make but one charge for any person who has revaccination attempted, no matter how often, if during the same epidemic or scare. Many people believe a vaccination protects as long as the scar shows plainly. The truth is a vaccine scar lasts for life, while the protective influence of vaccination gradually disappears in some people. A typical vaccine scar merely shows that vaccination once took properly, not that it still protects.

Some people think a revaccination must be made to take anyhow, even though they are still protected by the old one. You cannot catch fish when there are none, no matter how you bait your hook, nor set a pile of stones on fire, no matter how good the matches you use.

Another error regarding small-pox : Many people imagine that it can only thrive when the weather is cold ; this is a mistake, as it may prevail with intensity at any season. Indeed, severe epidemics of it often prevail in tropical countries where there is perpetual summer.

Be very cautious how you go out of your way to persuade people to let you remove warts, extract tumors, destroy nævi, efface tattoo marks, and do other minor surgical operations gratis, with assurances of success. There is always a remote possibility of serious or fatal sequelæ, and you should not, especially in private practice, induce people to let you involve yourself for their benefit, without being paid for your risk and responsibility: It is an ugly thing to have a wart you have insisted upon tampering with, become an ulcerating epithelioma. Indeed, it is better to avoid all unrequited work and all gratuitous responsibility, except what charity calls for.

For similar reasons do not persuade people to effect insurance on their lives, or in any particular company, as all such ventures carry a possibility of disappointment or failure that might involve you.

Wisdom in recognizing cases that are likely to involve you in suits for malpractice, and in foreseeing and forestalling the suits themselves, is a valuable power. Take care that this wisdom does not come too late, or cost you too much.

Never fail to send your bill promptly to dissatisfied patients, who are threatening to sue you for malpractice, or attempting to injure your practice unjustly, whether you expect them ever to pay it or not. If you cowardly shrink from sending your bill in such cases, they will quote that as a proof that you are guilty of what they charge, and that you know it; sending your bill gives you a better position before the public, and raises an issue that checkmates theirs. *Do not fail to charge the maximum fee in all such cases.*

Every principle of honor and duty forbids you even to think of lending yourself as a medical cat's-paw in unjust or speculative malpractice suits against physicians. Such self-styled " medical experts " often excite disgust and indignation at the contemptible attitudes they assume, when they act against their better knowledge and join hands with bad people and attempt to mulct a physician, or to clear a criminal from legal responsibility on the plea of " insanity," or other wicked absurdity gotten up to make money or to defeat justice.

Probably there is no department of professional duty in which physicians are so often asked to *stretch* their consciences, as that of giving certificates to persons seeking to get government pensions.

You may even be cajoled by friends or flattered by interested strangers, or tempted by gold, to give an opinion that one, who was mentally unfit to make a will, was fully able to do so, or that a person with one foot in the grave, the result of intemperance or disease, is sound or temperate, or that some one with a bias towards a certain disease, or with an incipient organic affection, is in perfect health. Or pleasure-seeking officials may attempt to cover their absence from duty by obtaining a certificate from you that their absence was due to sickness ; others may attempt through you to escape military or jury duty, or attendance at court as a witness, or for trial, or to get from you a prescription for a " Sunday drink of liquor" under the pretence of sickness.

Repel all such approaches promptly ; and emphatically refuse to stretch the truth, or to deviate from professional honor for any one.

Steer clear of this and all other practices and alliances in which your part would not bear legal scrutiny, or detailing in the community; and you will not only safely pass the shoals of shame and bitterness, upon which so many have been wrecked, but you will have a positive reward—the approval of your conscience.

CHAPTER III.

"Whatsoever a man soweth, that shall he also reap."—GAL. vi. 7.

When you are importuned to produce abortion, on the plea of saving the poor girl's character, or to prevent her sister's heart from being broken, or her father from discovering her misfortune and committing murder, or to prevent the child's father from being disgraced, or to avert the shame that would fall on the family, or the church scandal, or to limit the number of children for married people who already have as many as they want, or for ladies who assert that they are too sickly to have children, or that their suckling child is too young to be weaned, etc., etc., you should meet such entreaties and solicitations with a refusal prompt, chilling and emphatic, and never even seem to entertain the proposition. If they are too importunate, express your sentiments strongly.

How could any one but a fool be induced to take the burden from another's shoulders to his own, by doing a crimson crime; to violate both his conscience and the law; to risk exposure, social disgrace, and professional ruin, and even the penitentiary itself, by putting himself into any one's guilty power, whether as a favor or for a paltry fee?

Evil rumors fly rapidly. The production of a very few criminal abortions (sometimes even a single one) will

5

surely go from tongue to tongue, and give the foolish physician who stoops to commit them a widespread and long-continued notoriety as infamous and as tenacious as the Bloody Shirt of Nessus.

When circumstances require you to prescribe for females with delayed menses, where pregnancy is probably, or possibly the cause, it is better, instead of giving a Latinized prescription, to order some simple thing, such as hop tea, tincture of valerian, or wine of iron, under its common English name, and tell them verbally how to take it. By avoiding concealment regarding the nature of the remedies you give, you will escape the suspicion or charge of giving abortifacients.

You must give a cautious, a very cautious opinion, if any, in cases of unmarried females whose menses have ceased, and where pregnancy is feared; especially in cases where the suspected girl strenuously denies having had carnal intercourse. Erroneously to pronounce her pregnant may blast her whole future and call down maledictions on you; if on the contrary you too quickly declare her " not pregnant," it might injure you greatly; but this mistake would be nothing in comparison with the other. Temporize or suspend your opinion for weeks, or even months if need be, till positively certain by hearing the fœtal heart beat, or some other unequivocal sign.

Unmarried negresses and low females who fear they are pregnant, will occasionally come and consult you, consume your time and get your opinion, and when you discover that they are really pregnant, and refuse to produce abortion, will try to escape payment of your office fee.   In all such cases inform them at the beginning how much your fee is for your time, opinion and advice, and that it must be paid whether your recommendation agrees with their wishes or not.   After settling the fee question, study their case and give them your opinion and advice.

If you should ever encounter a case in which you believe the production of abortion is necessary to save the mother's life, do not consent to do it secretly, but only after consultation with some other physician of well-known probity.

Giving directions for the prevention of conception or instructing in onanism, or in the guilty use of syringes and other expedients to aid crime or to defeat nature, though offences beyond the reach of the laws, are derogatory and degrading to the physician and an abuse of his professional office.

Never carry away, or keep chloroform, ergot, splints, instruments, unused medicines, etc., that patients have paid for, without an agreement with them to that effect; and never partake of a sick man's wine or liquor, or eat his fruit and cake, etc.   To do such things would not only lay you open to criticism, but even to the most mortifying charges if a rupture of friendship should ever occur —in fact, with such things to fortify them, many people would be actually disposed to welcome, or create a rupture with you.

You should be careful that attempts to conceal the presence of contagious diseases, of unlawful dangers to health, or of births that result from clandestine marriage, or from bastardy, do not involve you in the exposures and recriminations that are apt to follow.

If you have skill in avoiding cases that would involve a summons to court as a witness, and kindred annoyances, legal and social, it will be the source of much comfort.

The practice of medicine isolates the members of our profession from one another much more than one would suppose. Physicians daily pass and repass each other without a look or nod; although fellow-workers in the profession and well known to each other by sight or reputation, and although acquaintanceship and social amenities would be mutually agreeable and beneficial and possibly ripen into life-long friendship, they often remain as strangers for years, unless accident brings them together.

Do not hold yourself aloof from the profession; but identify yourself with it in all public medical matters, at medical conventions, at assemblages of alumni, at medical meetings called to provide entertainment for visiting medical celebrities, to pay special tributes of respect to deceased medical brethren, at those held to voice the opinions or policy of the profession regarding public dangers or matters of hygiene, or to take action on epidemics, etc., etc.

Also, join the medical societies of your neighborhood; organization does good, both to the profession and to individuals. A good medical society is almost equal to a post-graduate school. Friction of mind in amicable discussion awakens reflection and deepest thought, which in turn increases the intellectual grasp and stimulates the mental digestive power, and they in turn liberalize and enlarge each one's scope and act as leaven to the entire profession. Nowhere else can you study so well the individuality and the styles of different physicians, and learn the secrets of each one's success or failure so fully, as at medical meetings. There the specialist, the teacher and the general practitioner all meet, and each in his own way contributes to the instruction and intellectual recreation of the others. There, you can meet your neighbors on common ground, and compare experience and opinion by face-to-face discussion. There, rivalries, dissensions and controversies can be softened, and professional friendships be formed; there, you can measure the height and depth of your medical contemporaries, and see the difference between the judicious and the injudicious, between intellectual giants and dwarfs; there, you can estimate the influence of the undefinable excellences of some, and discover and learn to avoid the glaring imperfections of others,—and in many other respects learn effectually to separate the chaff from the wheat.

Of course, medical societies are neither a specific for all personal deficiencies, nor a panacea for all professional sores. Spending a few hours among honorable physicians, once a week, will not convert a willing doer of evil into a professional Chesterfield, or give him the polish and value of refined gold, or lend him a conscience like Milton's, but it will serve as an intellectual and social exchange, where one may hear the discussion of moot points, and get therefrom new combinations of ideas and fresh streams of knowledge.

Beside the individual benefits accruing to the members, they as a body catch inspiration from the proceedings, which stimulates the healthy growth of the profession at large, and generates and fosters a genuine professional spirit that constantly tends to minimize all that is unprofessional.

Never oppose the admission of any one into society membership for private or personal reasons, or for any cause other than ineligibility or unfitness to receive the honors and benefits membership confers, because medical societies exist for the benefit of all regular physicians, and for the good of mankind, and it would be unjust to interpose an objection, or to cast a black ball against any one, on purely personal grounds.

Do not hesitate to take part in medical debates, whenever you have anything valuable to offer, whether gleaned from literature, or from the great school of experience. If you have a contribution to offer, a discovery to announce, or a new instrument to show, or an operation to describe, or a case or specimen to present, or anything at all to say, do it in a careful, methodical manner, then sit down; but always remember, that when you have nothing worth offering, silence should be your law—do not break it. In speaking, take care neither to abandon your medical vocabulary for the vernacular, nor let your professional manner degenerate. Remember there, as elsewhere, that there is nothing infallible; that a physician must school his prejudices and be open to conviction. Those who can brook no opinion that does not accord with their own, are usually hot-headed, rash and indiscreet, and very unsafe guides. Also, remember that controversies, discussions and parliamentary battles, no matter how sharp, are usually conducted by men of discretion within the bounds of decorum, and without violations of the ordinary rules of good breeding; that there is no mode of practice and no remedy for any disease which has not been the subject of obstinate dispute, and that every new discovery or announcement stirs the whole medical world to action, testing, reporting, asserting and denying.

You will find that many of the laity entertain a belief that medical societies exist for the pecuniary advancement of physicians, just as trades-unions and other organizations do for workingmen, and that they in some way, or to some extent, limit the freedom of personal opinion, and abridge the rights of their members. Be careful to correct such errors on all suitable occasions, and to inform those thus misled that medical societies exist not for selfish, but mainly for scientific purposes.

Keep up your medical studies, or the knowledge which you have already acquired will rapidly become misty and slip away from you. Without study, the details of cases and the symptoms of many diseases wear out of one's memory; indeed, the mind does not often bring back the details of parallel cases, or of cases for comparison, after two or three years have elapsed, unless they are extremely uncommon or interesting.

In consulting journals and text-books, remember that practice found successful in your own climate or region is usually more reliable for your use than that applicable in other climates. Avoid relying on antiquated works on practice and back volumes of journals, as guides in so progressive a science as medicine. New investigations and rapid progress render new text-books frequently necessary, to those who would maintain that buoyancy and self-reliance which the consciousness of being fully posted inspires.

Try to get together a library of useful books as soon as possible after graduating; money spent in this way will return a hundredfold. But take care that book-agents, with "the greatest work ever published," do not induce you by their importunities to subscribe for books for which you have but little or no use. No one can patronize everything, or even read one-tenth of all that is offered, unless he has nothing else to do.

Of course you should subscribe to as many good medical journals as you can afford to pay for, and read and digest them carefully, so as to keep abreast of the times; they are necessary to the progressive physician. But neither swear at, nor by, all you see in them; be especially careful of such as exist for the purpose of advertising either their owner or his goods. As a rule you will find that statements involving therapeutics found in the latest text-books, are more mature and more reliable than articles in journals, which are often founded on a single case, or the exaggerated fancy, or unconfirmed experience, or speculations of a single individual.

Do not be biased too quickly, or strongly, in favor of new or unsettled theories based on physiological, microscopical or chemical experiments; especially when offered by the over-zealous to prove their own hobbies or pet ideas.

Never abandon the practical branches of medicine for histology, pathology, microscopic anatomy, refined diagnostics, bacteriamania, and other subjects that merely interest, or it will impair your practical tendency and give you a wrong bias, and your usefulness as a practising physician will almost surely diminish.

I do not apply these remarks to teachers and experimenters, who have hospital and laboratory facilities, or are pursuing science chiefly to gain distinction therein, or solely as an object of pleasure, and who do not look to their practice for support. I mean to say that a person may get so deeply absorbed in science as to think of nothing but science, and that your most useful studies as a practitioner will be the practical, and above all else, the art of treating diseases with success.

Never publish weak or trifling medical articles, as whatever one writes is supposed to be a mirror of his own mind. Do not, however, hesitate to write whenever you have anything valuable or instructive to offer, either for the benefit of others or to increase your own standing and reputation.

When possible, base your articles on facts, or on an analysis of facts, rather than on speculation and theory. Let your diction be pure and simple, and as short and explicit as perspicuity will allow, so as not to weaken your ideas, observations or deductions, or obscure them in a lot of wordy trash.

Be careful to give your article a concise, appropriate and attractive title, one that indicates its contents, one that will show with sufficient clearness the general character of the remarks which are to follow. This is especially requisite when the title of the work is to be put in an index or catalogue. Such titles as "A Curious Case," "A New Method," etc., furnish no clue whatever.

In writing, cultivate simplicity of style, avoid diffuse-ness, and use no far-fetched quotations from foreign or dead languages, unless followed immediately by transla-tion; for unless it be some stale or hackneyed term, the average reader will probably be forced either to pass it over unsolved, or take down his dusty quotation book or his schoolboy grammar. The English language is capa-ble of expressing any and every thought, and it is a pity that from ignorance or pedantry some are unable to ex-press themselves in their mother-tongue. .

The recent attempt to supersede the old weights and measures by the metric system did not succeed; it is therefore scarcely worth while to weigh its merits. When you report cases or publish anything in which weights are given, either use the old familiar weights and measures (which every one understands), or give both the old and the metric; to use the metric only savors of pedantry. Many make no attempt to carry the metric equivalents in their minds, and if you give metric measures only they may pass your effusions by with-out getting the information you wish to convey.

Note all remarkable cases, but never report or pub-lish any that are not unique, or at least that do not present some curious, rare or very instructive feature, or militate against accepted theories; otherwise you will merely swell without adding anything valuable to ex-isting records. You will find every department of medi-cine fast becoming loaded down with theoretical discus-sions, speculative dissertations, compilations and empty word-building—old things said in a new form. You should contribute original work, and new ideas, if any.

Use a plain, intelligible style, and be as brief and concise as justice to your subject will allow, and, for the printer's sake, prepare your matter so as to require but little if any revision.

When you write essays or monographs, use for convenience sake the smallest sized sheets of white note paper; this will enable you to handle them more easily in writing, altering and re-writing pages, and also to carry and preserve them much better than if large. If intended for the press, write only on one side of the sheet, and leave a margin at the edge.

When you publish anything, do not follow the custom of appending to your name a long tail, consisting of all the titles and honors, whether strong or weak, that you can rake together, with half a dozen etc's; such an enumeration is in bad taste and excites the ridicule of discerning people. The idea governing the use of suffixes is chiefly that the individual who writes may be identified; a single suffix or simple title, or your town, street and number, are modest and yet sufficiently explicit.

Never furnish a report, statement, or opinion on any important case or subject for publication either in book, journal or newspaper, without a proviso that you are to see, and if necessary revise the proof and correct printer's errors in spelling, punctuation, etc., before it goes to press; otherwise you may find some purblind proofreader, or go-ahead printer, making you say the reverse of what you intended, thus necessitating a long list of " errata," or even making you regret that you ever allowed the article to appear in print.

Pay your honest debts punctually, even though you be cheated out of half you earn. The best plan is to pay as you go, and if you cannot pay much, do not go far. Owing for horses, carriages, feed, or clothes, or still worse, for luxuries, rent, servants' wages, etc., cannot fail to set the tongue of scandal to wagging freely and injuriously, to the possible ruin of your credit. You will have to pay every debt one time or another, and had better be paying each as it becomes due, than those that should have been paid a month or a year ago.

Borrowing books, instruments, umbrellas, money, etc., especially if you keep them beyond the proper time, or return them in bad condition, will tend to depreciate you more than you would think. Never involve yourself by borrowing apparatus, instruments, etc., from one physician, or patient, to lend to another; if necessary, introduce the parties, and let the borrower do the borrowing on his own responsibility.

Guard against repulsive habits; do not squirt tobacco-juice around you at your visits, or have your breath reeking with its fumes, or with those of cloves, cardamom, alcohol, dead beer, etc., or you will unavoidably invite criticism and create revulsion towards you.

Appearing in your shirt sleeves, wearing rough, creaking boots, or chewing, smoking, sky-larking, etc., will show weakness, diminish your prestige, detract from your dignity and lessen you in public esteem, by forcing on everybody the conclusion that you are after all but an ordinary person.

Carpentering, painting, or showing other common-place or out-of-place talents, will also appear as if your mind was not engrossed by your profession. You may possibly secure faith in spite of these, but usually such things tend decidedly to decrease it.

Drunkenness may be tolerated in physicians who are fully established in practice, because friendly attachments had been formed and their talents and worth had become known previous to the formation of the habit; but it is fatal to the prospects of a beginner.

An excellent course is to avoid intoxicating drinks yourself, and let others do as they think best. If it is known that you never drink, it will be of immense advantage to your reputation; but intemperately urging temperance on all occasions, or being a member of temperance, of secret, or of beneficial societies, will not aid much in the acquirement of desirable business; indeed, the best practice you can have is the quiet family business that you will attract by faithful endeavors to do your best for all who apply to you.

Temperance, total abstinence, prohibition, and other sumptuary crusades will be apt to recoil on your head, if you make yourself prominent in them. Pushing matters of a partisan or secular nature is not your function, and you cannot become officious in them without engendering rancorous enemies. You had better leave all such matters to the laity, unless your pecuniary or social position is such that you can very well afford it, or you are driven into them by conscientious scruples that outweigh all other considerations; and even then, it is better to let your profession be foremost in your mind.

Presents from fond or grateful, very liberal or romantically generous patients, although flattering, will almost invariably lead to the disarrangement or actual rupture of the legitimate pecuniary relations previously existing between yourself and the giver, which it may consequently be impossible fully to restore. Probably every practitioner can recall numerous instances in which presents of knee-blankets, whips, game, fruit, cigars, wine, pet animals, canes, free passes, gloves, new hats, curiosities, etc., have proved exceedingly expensive. When you foresee such a result, be guarded.

A good rule is to decline all presents that would place you under embarrassing obligations to patients. Another good rule is to avoid mixed dealings and crossed accounts with hucksters, grocers, feed-men, milk-men, and other patients, as such an arrangement will rarely continue to be satisfactory; it often engenders disagreements, and will almost always result in your getting only about half as much for your services as if you had avoided entanglements. It is decidedly better to conduct affairs upon strictly business principles, *i. e.*, let those for whom you work pay you in money, you in turn doing the same. In a word, avoid everything that tends to weaken your business rules.

Preserve a proper degree of gravity and dignity on all occasions. Frivolous conduct, vulgar jokes, great levity and undue familiarity are unprofessional, and breed contempt and scandal. Discourage all attempts to rudely address you with a " Hallo, Doc !" or by your first name, or to pass the limit of propriety in any way with you. Give every one his proper title, and exact the same respect in return. Do not understand me to condemn good-natured pleasantry; when manly and within bounds, it is often very appropriate, and sometimes actually serves as a tonic to a patient's drooping spirits. If you have a becoming earnestness of deportment, and at the same time wear a cheerful mien, it will be health to you and sunshine to your patients.

Avoid dining out with patients, attending their tea or card parties, etc. Eat as seldom as possible at their houses—only when unavoidably detained there by cases of labor, convulsions and the like. There is a tendency to conviviality and *abandon* around the festive board that has a leveling effect, and divests the physician of his proper prestige. Better to eat a cold repast at home than to partake of the most savory viands of many a patient. Let a physician once unbend among certain kinds of patients, and he risks a complete loss of their esteem.

When compelled to accept a meal, if you are served alone, so much the better ; if seated to eat with the household, be courteous but somewhat reserved, and exhibit only enough of the social element to be agreeable. Shun *badinage* and gossip, and over-praising of the viands, and avoid speaking afterwards of the " snowy biscuits," or the " delicious butter," " the juicy beefsteak," etc., as though you were a stranger to choice food.

Try to give satisfaction at your visits; show that you are anxious to relieve both the body and mind of your patient, and you will not—cannot fail to succeed in your ambition to get practice. To do this fully you must, of course, feel and express a genuine interest in the case, and in the effects of the remedies you are using.

When you scold or find fault with patients or their attendants, preface what you say by explaining that you are *not scolding in anger,* but because you feel an earnest desire to have them do right for everybody's sake. By prefacing thus you will completely disarm resentment, and they will take all you say in good part.

If you are unmarried, it will often be quoted against you; but the truth is, there is no great professional advantage gained by being married. The objection to most unmarried physicians is really not their celibacy, but their youthfulness. To marry with an eye to business only, would be apt to entail expenses and responsibilities without corresponding benefits. Besides, you should keep both business and marriage on a higher plane. You will often see in your professional career the misery that flows from degrading marriage by entering into it from other considerations than love and congeniality, and you should not risk it yourself.

Everybody wants a lucky, conservative physician; therefore a series of dystocias, or of deaths in child-bed, or of surgical operations that fail, or of malignant cases, or of cases of any kind that eventuate unexpectedly ill, often injures the physician for years, by attaching to him—especially if he be a beginner—either charges of being blind to danger and to duty, or a *long-to-be-re-membered* reputation for bad luck. If such a series unfortunately threatens you in the beginning of your practice, strengthen yourself by consultations, etc.

The power of impressing those you meet with a favorable opinion of your adaptation to your calling, is an important advantage. Discipline yourself by self-examination, whenever you have conducted yourself unsatisfactorily. This will teach you to conceal, or eradicate your defects and faults, and to give prominence to your good qualities.

No one can succeed fully without the favorable opinion of the maids and matrons he meets in the sickroom. They can be his best friends or his worst enemies. The females of every family have a potent voice in selecting the family physician. I have often thought that the secret why so many truly scientific aspirants fail to get practice is, that cold logic and rigid mathematics and other high theoretical attainments, however much admired, are often attained at the expense of the endearing sentiments, and hence excite no sympathy, but, on the contrary, are often associated with a deficiency of those minor qualities of head and heart which appeal to the female mind and work upon its emotional element.

Ability to please and retain those who employ you in an emergency, or tentatively, is also a power that you should carefully cultivate.

You will find that remembrance of the names of children and of patients whom you see but rarely, and the ability to recall the salient points of former interviews with them, are very useful adjuncts to other qualities.

Children's likes and dislikes will control your destiny in many a family. Many people patronize various forms of quackery for no greater reason than that "the children take it easily," knowing from experience, that an attempt to give pills or bitter doses to refractory or spoilt children means a fight and a failure.

You must not rely strongly on social influence for

6

getting practice. Your very best friends may prefer that you test your skill and gain your experience on others, rather than on them or theirs.

You may be socially a great favorite while all are well, but when sickness comes and death threatens the afflicted one, the impulses of friendship are dormant and do not influence the choice of a physician. No member of any family circle will be spared, if any human power can save, and persons terrified at the possibility of losing the provident husband, beloved wife, blooming daughter, darling babe, dutiful son, or honored parent, as the case may be, instinctively send for the doctor in whose skill they have most confidence. They go past the beginner, about whom they know too little,—past the one whose system requires so much stimulating, about whom they know too much,—past the gay, the fickle, the sentimental, and the unchaste,—past all whose unprofessional demeanor proves them to be either unripe, or unsuited to a stewardship so solemn, so precious, so weighty as that of a family physician,—past all, till they reach the one in whom their faith, their medical confidence centres; faith is the great controlling lever.

Be polite and considerate to every one, especially when you are vexed or in a hurry; abruptness makes many useless wounds, some of which are difficult to heal. True politeness is a seed that costs nothing, can be planted anywhere—that always bears good fruit. Resolve that you will cultivate it as long as you live.

When boys or young men come to you for assistance for their Base Ball Clubs, or their library, and the like, give something and give it freely. If ladies ask you for a donation to aid the heathen (!!!) or to help buy a carpet for their church, or any other laudable object, give willingly and cheerfully. If the tiny boy or girl comes to sell a concert or festival ticket, buy it laughingly, for contributions this way not only do good, but have other consequences. Were you to scowl and say "no," the young man and woman and the tiny boy would unite in calling you " old stingy," and ever after avoid you.

There is a certain fact that you might not observe without having your attention called to it; it is, that after you get into full practice, your days, weeks, months and years will flit by faster than those of other people, because as a physician they will be incessantly engrossed with a medley of important cases, and the lapse of time will consequently be almost magical.

You should get as much out of life as you can by seeking proper relaxations and amusements while the age for enjoying them remains. Many physicians, in the eager pursuit of business, foolishly postpone all relaxation from one time to another, intending to indulge in ease and social amenities and to pursue the pleasures of life when they get older; they thus forego seeking enjoyments till they lose all taste for them, till they know nothing and are fit for nothing but to plod in the physician's hard, slavish treadmill for life.

It is asserted that working seven days in a week shortens a life of threescore and ten by twenty years.

A little leisure is a great blessing. Do as little work on Sundays and holidays as possible. An occasional day's sport with rod or gun, or a summer trip, or an evening at a convivial gathering, or at the theatre, etc., will act as seasoning to your labors, lessen the worries

and cares of practice, break the monotony of life,
subdue irritability, the result of overwork, conduce to
longevity, and actually make you more philosophical
and a better physician.

Newspaper notices of your departure from the city
for short seaside, mountain, or other brief pleasure trips,
will, if allowed, have a disturbing and hurtful influence
on your practice while you are away, and even after
your return. Reporters are aware how such items injure physicians, and seldom publish them unless requested. The register clerk of hotels where you
register will, if asked to do so, omit announcing your
arrival in the newspapers, which would publish your
absence from business to the whole world.

After prolonged absence from home, or recovery from
long sickness, it is perfectly ethical to announce the fact
of your return to practice through the newspapers:
Dr. ———— will resume practice at his office, No.—
street, July 1st, 1885.

When you assume charge of a case for another physician, to look after during his absence from the city, or
one of your own that has been under the care of a substitute while you were away, or that any one has attended in an emergency pending your arrival, or because the attending physician has been taken sick, continue his line of treatment, at least for a while, if you can
conscientiously do so. An abrupt radical change, either
in diagnosis, prognosis or treatment, is both ungenerous
and injurious to your co-worker. In such a case, if you
believe something more should be given, merely add it
to what is already being done. This avoids unpleasant
reflections.

CHAPTER IV.

Always feel and show respect for your seniors in practice. There is probably no type of medical man so unworthy of respect as the one who shows contempt for his seniors. You may excel the older physicians in severely scientific and technical points, but experience has been their teacher, and they have a ripe clinical acquaintance with disease, and an intuitive perception as to the choice of remedies which in general makes them better logicians and much better practitioners, because knowledge and skill derived from observation and experience far outweigh mere book knowledge, are more like part of one's very nature than that gotten from any other source, and are fixed indelibly on both one's senses and reason, to be brought forth again when needed. Remember that although young physicians indulge more than older ones in scientific " extras," and modern instrumental aids to diagnosis, yet relying on these too much and studying rational symptoms too little, they seem to forget that the art of curing disease owes more to good judgment and sound common-sense bedside observation and experience than to anything else.

The older practitioner is more apt to slight the nicer pathological diagnosis, which discovers the technical character of the disease—whether, for instance, a pneu-

monia is catarrhal, croupous or interstitial—and to attend
more to the therapeutical diagnosis which indicates
what the treatment should be; weighing the influence
of age, season, rate of progress, secondary affections, compensatory changes, and other phenomena with a nicety
that the junior can never learn from his books, then
choosing with intuitive wisdom the best remedies for the
discomforts, annoyances, and sufferings of the patient;
reducing, evacuating, quieting, stimulating, or feeding
him, as experience has taught. Such men do very much
to give our profession honorable standing, and are certainly worthy of all respect.

When you have been a physician long enough to make
your patients feel that you have a judgment of your
own and evolve it out of your own brain, and that you
alone are acquainted with their moral and physical
idiosyncrasies, it will give you great advantage, and
will make attending them much easier. You will occasionally be employed in cases because you have long ago
attended other members of the family in similar affections, and are supposed to know the family constitution,
temperament and tendencies, and to possess sovereign
remedies for their relief.

You will find that the popular belief that you know
this or that person's constitution, and know exactly what
they require, and their likes and dislikes, is a powerful acquisition, one that gives you great authority, and
gives them unquestioning confidence.

Experience and skill are what the public seek in a
physician; they are most important, and everybody
knows it. You should carefully try to appear possessed

of both. Of course, we all have aftersight, but foresight is what is needed. This is sure to come from practical experience in diagnosticating and combating disease, and will develop and improve your judgment in every way, and enable you each year to foresee events with increased clearness; and if you compel yourself to work faithfully and to develop the faculty of observing, every year will make you a better physician, and by the time you have worked and observed for ten or twelve years, you will be clinically familiar with all the more common afflictions that are sure to confront you, and you will know from experience how to avoid various errors and mistakes, and how to shape your diagnosis, prognosis and treatment in each, far better than your juniors.

In addition to the great advantage the older physicians have over the younger ones, from increased ability to foresee the probable degree and duration of grave cases, and to give concerning them more definite and truer opinions from the beginning, they can from experience recognize and point out cases that are dubious or likely to prove very slow and tedious, thereby saving themselves from much anxiety and blame. Of course, these advantages advance their reputation, give them greater confidence in themselves, and enable them to carry cases with greater steadiness and to retain confidence much better than younger physicians. This is the chief reason why older physicians are not harassed in difficult cases by meddling officiousness from outsiders, and dismissed, or forced to call consultations, as often as younger ones, and why the practice of medicine becomes relatively easier every year. You will find that after you have practised twelve or fifteen years, after you have forgotten much of your theoretical knowledge,—which was probably greater comparatively at graduation than it will ever be again,—your experience will be invaluable to you, and will often serve you where book-learning cannot; indeed, it is impossible to obtain from books alone sufficient knowledge of disease to become a good practitioner. Self-attained post-graduate knowledge is the kind that makes the public prefer older physicians to younger ones.

The public love to see a physician appear to understand his business fully, to know things intuitively; therefore you must study and practise to be quick in diagnosis, and ever ready in the treatment of the ordinary cases that will constitute nine-tenths of your practice.

Study the laws of prognosis and duration continually, for it is in these that most error is seen. Very few people can discover whether or not your diagnosis and treatment are correct, but if you say a patient will recover and he dies, or that he will die and he gets well, or that he will be sick a month and he gets up in three days, or that he will be well in three days and he is sick a month, everybody will see that you are wrong, and will very naturally infer, that as you were wrong in your prognosis, you might also have been wrong in your diagnosis and treatment.

Skill in these things will enable you to foretell a favorable, a doubtful, or a fatal termination, and to foreknow the duration in a greatly increased proportion of your cases, and save you a vast amount of anxiety.

In forming your prognosis be careful to ascertain, not

only the condition of the organ chiefly diseased, but that of all the other vital organs, as their condition and action may, in some measure, compensate for the lost functions of the diseased organ. Look also at the surroundings of your patient, and the nursing and attention he can command; and lastly, learn to estimate, from the look, voice, gesture and general aspect, mental and physical, his vital resistance to the disease (which differs in each individual), and then form your prognosis.

Never ask, as you enter to pay the first visit to a patient, the awkward question, "What is the matter with you?" or at any other visit, "How are you to-day?" or he may retort, *that* is exactly what he wants the physician to tell him.

Never display the fact that you are a junior working by reflected light, and thereby belittle yourself in the estimation of patients, by constantly quoting what the books say, or what such-and-such a medical celebrity says.

The folly of blindly accepting, or slavishly following the dicta of others, is nicely depicted by Molière in *L'Amour Médécin*, Acte ii, Scène 2, where the following dialogue occurs between Dr. Tomès and Lisette:

Tomès.—How is the coachman?

Lisette.—He is dead.

Tomès.—Dead?

Lisette.—Yes.

Tomès.—That is impossible.

Lisette.—It may be impossible, but it is so.

Tomès.—He cannot be dead, I say.

Lisette.—I tell you he is dead and buried.

Tomès.—You are mistaken.

Lisette.—I saw it.

Tomès.—It is impossible. Hippocrates says that such diseases do not terminate till the fourteenth or twenty-first day, and it is only six days since he was taken sick.

Lisette.—Hippocrates may say what he pleases, but the coachman is dead.

Take a lesson from this and remember that your patients, whether bankers, mechanics, laborers, or women, want to know what *you* think, and care but little for Hippocrates, Watson, Gross, or Ringer.

If you are determined to let people know you are inexperienced and have no opinion of your own, you should at least spare them the infliction of following you to the sources from, and through the processes by which your borrowed opinions were obtained.

If one is invited to dinner, he may imagine his host does not prepare it all himself, but he does not care to be taken by his host down into the kitchen and through the pantries, and shown his pots and pans and rolling pins, and to be introduced to the cooks and waiters, all to let him know exactly how the feast is prepared. One will feel much better entertained if he is, at the proper time, simply introduced to the table, smoking and groaning with its bounteous supply

Remember this : every one likes to believe that the physician is treating him by a regular plan rather than firing at random, more especially in diseases that are believed to depend on the blood or on a diathesis.

Make post-mortem examinations, and other scientific

use of your opportunities whenever proper cases present themselves, but never allow the inference that you are doing so to gratify idle curiosity, or to satisfy yourself alone, or that it is a very great favor to be allowed to do it; rather put it on the higher ground that it is for the benefit of science, and in the interest of suffering humanity, and it may be for the good of the very persons with whom you are talking.

It is, of course, wrong, very wrong, to consent to make a post-mortem examination of any one who has died under the care of another physician, at the solicitation of those who seek to disprove the diagnosis and disgrace the medical attendant.

The hypostatic congestion that naturally follows death is often mistaken by the public for ante-mortem changes, and gives rise to the most wonderful stories of "murder," "only in a trance," etc. Take care to inform people of its nature and cause, and its utter lack of significance.

Experiments that require vivisection of animals will not add much to your reputation, if done with that in view, as such things are supposed to have been studied as far as needful before leaving college. On the contrary, making clinical analyses of the urine and other fluids will not only lead you to invaluable information regarding your patient's condition, but will be a great element in giving you popularity and respect.

Working with the microscope on proper occasions will not only increase your knowledge, but will also invest you with the benefits of a scientific reputation in public esteem.

Obstetrical practice is in some respects desirable,

especially in the beginning, as it paves the way to permanent family practice. *Doing the waiting* at the bedside, however, entails a tremendous loss of time. Chance calls of any kind you can take or not at your option, whereas engagements, especially obstetrical ones, must be kept, day or night.

If you ever get so overrun with business that time is precious with you, having many obstetrical cases will overtax you, and it may become actually necessary, in self-defence, to shut off these and other engrossing engagements, to get time to attend the rest of your patients with something like regularity, and to obtain your meals, sleep, etc.; or, at least, to limit such engagements as much as possible. Midwifery is a wearing, exhausting branch of medicine, one that is full of care and responsibility; and although it leads to other family practice, you will find after some years that the ordinary fees for attending cases of confinement are, on account of loss in waiting and consequent interference with other engagements and duties, and on account of the fatigue and want of sleep, etc., which they occasion, proportionately more meagre than in any other department of practice.

If you keep a record you will probably find that nine-tenths of all your loss of rest is due to obstetrical cases.

When a person engages you to attend her in confinement, write her call on one of your cards and give it to her, and instruct her to send it to you as soon as she feels that you are needed. This emphasizes the engagement, and makes her more apt, when her time comes, to call you in, than to employ another physician, or to get a midwife.

In spite of your having been engaged for a case, and kept in suspense for weeks or months, you will sometimes learn that the confinement is over, that a midwife or granny was sent for, and the excuse will be that everything occurred in such a hurry that they could not wait for you, or that they had no messenger, or some other equally lame plea.

You will often be called upon in bad cases to do ugly work for midwives who have reached the limit of their skill, and for the sufferer's sake you should never refuse to go.

Such occasions will afford you an excellent chance to show the advantages regular physicians have over midwives and irregulars, and also to enhance yourself in public esteem.

Pregnant women will sometimes want to make an Indian bargain with you beforehand, to come to them in case their midwife fails. Of course you should go to all cases where humanity calls, but you should never bargain with anybody beforehand to play second part to a midwife—she to take the fee and the éclat, if there is no trouble, you to take the care and responsibility for a nominal fee, if there is. You may be surprised to learn that it is now generally understood in many communities, that every midwife has her regular medical referee to relieve her of complicated cases—a one-sided bargain, which gives him an undue proportion of worrying cases.

In every confinement case, after delivering the child, be careful to call the mother's attention to the lump in her abdomen, and inform her that it is only the contracted uterus. If you do not, she may accidentally discover it, get greatly alarmed, and either await your visit in terror, or send for you post-haste.

Attending very distant patients of any kind has a tendency to disorganize and diminish one's nearer practice; for while absent, attending a remote call, you may lose three nearer ones. A long visit does not, as a rule, pay pecuniarily, and is an injustice to both physician and patient. Every one should have a family physician within reasonable calling distance. A few far-off patients will waste more time, break down more horseflesh, use up more carriages, harass you more at unseasonable hours, and expose you to bad weather more, than all the remainder of your practice.

Keep your practice down to a number which you can attend properly; you can do this by sending your bills promptly, by weeding out worthless patients, by circumscribing your bounds, cutting off obstetrical engagements, raising your fees, etc. In refusing to take a case at a distance, or one that is likely to involve you as a witness in court against your will, or to engage for midwifery, if you are "*too busy*," name that as your chief reason, as it is the least open to criticism and over-persuasion of any that can be assigned.

Never offer as an excuse for neglect to visit a patient, "I really forgot you"; it is unpardonable.

Gonorrhœal and syphilitic cases are not especially desirable on any account, except for the fees they bring; they are dirty, secret cases, and rather repel than attract their victims and their friends to the physician who attends them, when they require a physician for other diseases. Attending them will, however, often enable you to pick up a handsome cash office-fee.

Even when you are positive that a person has syphilis, it is not always best to say so. Prudence will sometimes require you to reserve your opinion, but at the same time give the proper medicine. Indeed, in practising medicine, you will see and understand many sins and blemishes of which you must appear oblivious.

Take care that your reputation for special interest in venereal diseases does not overshadow or eclipse other kinds, and give you the title of "P—x Doctor," and entail the social ostracism and loss of family practice that would follow; or that extra success in restoring the menses in females who suspect pregnancy, does not bring you an extra number of such cases, and give you the title of "Abortionist"; or that attending an excessive proportion of courtezans, or bruisers, does not give you the name of having a "fancy practice"; or that perpetual and indiscriminate inquiring about the urine, and having it bottled for you, does not earn for you the easily acquired title of "P—ss Doctor"; or that a liver hobby, or a kidney hobby, or the womb, or the stomach, does not become with you a scapegoat to be blamed for every obscure disease, and eventually lessen your usefulness and injure your character as a practitioner.

You will find it much more pleasant to practise in some families than in others; for some will constantly give you intelligent co-operation, and will make charitable allowance for all your shortcomings and failures, while others will, when any of their members are sick, appear almost as if they wanted to involve and harass

you in every conceivable way, and to make you feel as
though, in attending them, you were on trial for your
life.

It is this feeling of personal involvement and perpetual
anxiety, as much as over-work, that breaks down the
health and shortens the lives of physicians. Remember
this, and, like a philosopher, make it a rule never to
worry about anything you cannot help.

Be guarded against asking private questions before
persons not in the patient's confidence, unless they are
clearly entitled to hear them; request all such, especially if they are of the opposite sex, to leave the room
before asking. Be doubly cautious in this respect when
your patient is a female, and the questions refer to marriage, menstruation, pregnancy, lactation, uterine affections, constipation, urination, or other delicate subjects,
that her secrets may not be exposed, or her modesty
shocked.

Also avoid inquiring of a patient in stores or barber
shops, or on the street, in the presence of strangers,
about his ailments, or about patients at his home. Many
persons are very sensitive concerning their ailments, and
captious concerning the time, place and manner of asking about them.

Do not allow indiscreet patients to go about over-
praising you, and speaking of you as a pet, etc. Inor-
dinate praise, no matter from whom, is apt to arouse a
corresponding dislike on the part of those who deem the
praise either extravagant or misplaced; such injudicious praise will almost surely react against you, and
might even arouse the angriest jealousy on the part of

husbands, aunts, lovers, or others. Perfectly pure physicians have actually had to cease attending in families where such jealousy existed, to prevent causing domestic strife and estrangement.

It is also in bad taste, and even injurious, for any one to have wife, or other near relative, praising him inordinately, and boasting of his great skill and wonderful cases to all whom she meets, as people naturally think it colored by interested motives. If done at all, it comes with a great deal more grace from strangers.

Probably one of the greatest fortes you could possess is the power of discovering who are the *ruling spirits* in a family, and securing their faith and keeping them satisfied with you and your services.

Refuse to be confidential with curious or stupid nurses, or prying mischief-makers; and if you must answer their questions, do so, not in confidential whispers, but openly and in your ordinary voice.

As a rule, it is better in the family group to lend attention at your visits, chiefly to the conversation of the husband, if he is present, rather than to the wife, and to address your opinions, explanations and remarks to him, or whoever is at the head of those whom you meet in the sick-room, and to pay to all others only the respect that civility requires. If you do not do this, sensitive people will feel ignored, and many will even get dissatisfied and create trouble.

In visiting, banish all else from your mind but the case before you; and no matter who is present, make the patient, whether young or old, the central object, and keep your thoughts and your conversation on him

7

and his case. Both patients and their friends will naturally be more anxious to know what you think of their cases, and to receive information for their benefit, than to hear of anything else. If the conversation digresses to other subjects, shift it back to your patient and his case as soon as possible. During consultations also observe the same caution, and keep the conversation between you and your colleague on the case under consideration, and do not allow it to digress to religion, horses, politics, etc.; economy of time requires it, besides it is for that you are employed. Another fact to be kept in mind is this: if a consultation lasts too long, it is apt either to terrify the patient and his friends, or induce a belief that you disagree, or are puzzled, either of which may undo you.

Shrewdness in changing either a diagnosis or prognosis is very necessary in all cases where a change must be made.

Do not bind yourself too quickly or too closely in prognosticating the duration of a patient's case. Whatever prognosis you foreshadow in the beginning is, as a rule, accepted. It is only when that prognosis is changed to greater gravity, or its duration made much longer, that discontent arises. One of the strongest reproaches to medicine is, that it is not an *exact* science, therefore its practice often lacks the element of certainty.

Do not get insulted at the foibles and infirmities of the sick. Bear with the rude treatment you will occasionally receive from hysterical, peevish, or low-spirited patients, and do not take anything a sick or silly person says as an insult, unless you believe it is deliberately intended as such.

Beware of confidants. Never become so fond of patients, or any one else, as to make them the repository either of your professional or personal secrets. With our imperfect therapeutical means we cannot always attain perfect results, or give complete satisfaction, and some of those whom you have served most faithfully, and who you think will never change, will surprise and shock you by turning viciously against you and decrying you loudly. Bear the possibility of this ever in mind, and while making your relations with your friends and patients cordial, frank and free, always avoid telling secrets and making confessions that would put you into their power, if a rupture of friendship should ever occur.

To be over-assiduous in paying visits, when no sufficient cause is apparent, or to be too deferential and over attentive to those who think themselves extra good patients, is dangerous; for as soon as one imagines he is the best patient you have, or that you are cultivating him unnecessarily, he is sure to undervalue you and is apt to quit you.

When urgent necessity or danger requires it, you may do the most menial work for a patient; but unless these exist, pulling off your coat or collar, administering injections, giving baths, swaddling new-born babes, nursing the sick, rummaging drawers or ransacking cupboards in search of towels, old muslin for bandages, spoons, goblets, etc., does not comport with your position, and it may be quoted as evidence that you are without dignity and lack proper self-respect.

It is much better to ask for things you need, and have them brought to you.

A patient who is improving will be satisfied with a much shorter visit, slighter examination, and less perfect attention in general, than one who is not doing well, especially if he is doing so well that you can express your emphatic satisfaction with his progress, as you leave.

When a case is obscure, or in the initial stages, be cautious in expressing any positive or unguarded opinion; but in cases where you can safely do so, give an unequivocal, frank, free diagnosis and prognosis that express your full opinion. The habit of stating your views candidly will compel you to analyze closely, will discipline your judgment, and force you to study your cases and formulate opinions, instead of lumping everything and treating the patient for his most prominent symptoms, without stopping to notice or study the minor ones—as is done by mere routinists.

Remember that, contrary to popular belief, the art of medicine does not enable you, or any one else, to diagnosticate any of the eruptive fevers positively, till their local manifestations appear.

Frequently when a case is grave and you are being importuned to know whether you cannot do more, it is better casually to mention the things you deem contraindicated,—leeching, cupping, mustard, rubbing, baths, poultices, mopping the throat, electricity, etc., and tell why you have not ordered them, so as to let it be known you are wide awake and have thought of them, but have good reasons for not using them.

Never pronounce any one's sickness feigned or trifling, unless absolutely positive that it is so, and never make fun of people sending for you, or being alarmed at what appear to be trifling ailments or simple growths; indeed, you should never joke, talk frivolously, or laugh about your patients or their sicknesses, either in their presence or elsewhere, and never taunt them about the trifling nature of their diseases. Some people will laugh off such a criticism, while secretly they feel hurt and resolve never to have you again. Another reason is that trifling ailments sometimes become serious diseases, and simple growths sometimes put on malignancy, and their becoming so *through fatal loss of time* is apt to be blamed on the joker for life.

Never guarantee a cure, or certain success, or a sure recovery, even for a mosquito bite; guarantee nothing, except that you know your duty and will do it. Medicine is not a perfect science, and life is not a definite quantity. When pressed to say whether any case of sickness is dangerous, reply promptly, "Of course there may be danger, *because* it is sickness, and any sickness, even a fly bite or a pin scratch, may become dangerous," and that even a well person has no guarantee of life from one day to another. Also remind the questioner, that you do not keep the book of life, that your will and God's will may differ, and that you cannot guarantee that any case of sickness may not become dangerous, or not have an unfavorable issue and even end in death; then tell him what you think will be the issue in the case in point. Remember, even in doing this, that while every case presents a scale of probabilities, it is surrounded by a group of possibilities, and do not fail to mention this fact, and to leave yourself a reasonable margin for uncertainties.

In giving death certificates in mania-a-potû, syphilis, abortion, etc., never yield to importunities, or a false tenderness for family affliction, and substitute other pleasant-sounding terms that risk putting you in a false position.

The laws everywhere confer on physicians honors and judicial powers that are refused to other classes. You are exempted from military and jury duty, and made an officer of the law regarding insanity, vaccination, etc., and your certificate regarding deaths, births, inability to attend court, and numerous other offices of permanent trust, are everywhere respected, and it is your duty in return to comply cheerfully and promptly with all legal requirements—to aid, rather than hinder enforcement of the laws.

In giving certificates, it is best to certify, "In my opinion," etc. Indeed, it is wiser, as well as more modest, in expressing an opinion, whether written or oral, to always say, "I believe thus and so," or "In my opinion," etc. The fact that it is your belief, or opinion, no one can dispute, even though it should prove erroneous.

Be exceedingly cautious in giving certificates of insanity, with a view to committing patients to an insane asylum. Do not yield to the importunity of mistaken or designing persons and commit the cruelty of depriving a poor fellow of his rights, liberty and property, because he entertains some harmless crotchet, as, for instance, that he is a tea-pot, or that his legs are of glass, or that some lady of high rank is in love with him, while in all other respects he is sane and conducts himself and manages his property rightly. Distinguish between the truly insane as contemplated by law, and those who may only seem to be insane. Dissatisfied friends of such people sometimes give great trouble to accommodating physicians in these cases. Give certificates in none but clear cases, and keep a memorandum of all the facts in each.

Also keep memoranda and observe great caution when you are a witness in will cases, suits for divorce, etc., to protect yourself against traitorous friends and designing enemies.

Remember that you are legally as well as morally bound to vaccinate a person after promising to do so. Besides the regrets and harsh criticism your neglect will generate, a suit for damages may follow if the patient gets small-pox while awaiting the fulfillment of your promise.

Never conceal the presence of a contagious disease from those around who are liable to contract it, or you may encounter the condemnation of the whole community. You will be apt to meet with rank opposition to your views when your decisions concerning the presence of, or danger from, cases of infectious diseases (smallpox, scarlatina, typhus fever, etc.), militate against the wishes or supposed interests of landlords, storekeepers, boarding-house mistresses, etc. In such cases do not be browbeaten into allowing any one to violate the laws relating to the public health. Your duty to the well is quite as great as to the diseased. Indeed, the public health is of far greater importance than the well-being of any individual.

When these or any other dilemmas present themselves, adopt Davy Crockett's wise motto, " Be sure you are right, then go ahead."

Carefully prevent children in whose family contagious disease exists, from infecting others by attending school, or otherwise mingling with those liable to contract it from them. Insist upon visitors being excluded from such cases. Also take care that its presence in hotels, stores, etc., is not kept secret at the public risk.

Never let people know that you are just from a case of smallpox, scarlet fever, measles, etc., or that you are even attending any contagious disease, or you will be credited with causing whatever cases occur among those whom you thus inform. If your practice is so full of such cases that you must tell it to somebody, tell the health authorities; indeed, the public good requires that you inform them anyhow.

After visiting contagious diseases, take care to disinfect your clothes by walking in the open air; also wash your hands with very hot water, or hold them over the fire; also use disinfecting lotions, etc., according to apparent need; if necessary, take a warm bath, or even a Turkish bath.

Oppose the conveyance of diphtheria, scarlet fever, measles, smallpox, cholera, yellow fever, typhus fever and other contagious diseases, in hacks, cars, and other public vehicles; and forbid the attendance of friends at the funerals of those who have died of such diseases, on the ground that the dead must not be allowed to kill the living.

Never keep a tongue-depressor for indiscriminate use, for besides the disgust which patients feel at having an instrument that has been used on everybody, put into their mouths, it might actually convey syphilis, diphtheria, etc., from one patient to another, and render you liable to just censure. When you wish to examine a throat at the patient's home, it is better to ask the nurse for a clean spoon, than to take a tongue-depressor from your pocket and excite the patient's disgust, and a lively curiosity among all around, to know when and upon what kind of a case it was last used. At your office an ivory paper-folder answers very well, is not disgusting, and is easily kept clean.

Do not lend yourself too freely to other physicians and surgeons; never make a habit of belittling yourself by giving chloroform, etc., in *surgical* cases. There is a great difference between giving assistance in medical and in surgical cases. If you visit a *medical* case with another physician, you will be regarded as a consultant, and as being at least equal, if not superior to him; besides, a fee may await you. If, on the contrary, you go and do some *secondary* part in a *surgical* case, you will be looked upon as a lesser light to the person whom you assist, and you will take a position neither of honor nor profit, and will reap nothing but responsibility. Do not habitually play the part of utility-man, or unpaid assistant, to any one except to your father or preceptor; servility and obsequiousness will never advance you, either in the community or in the profession.

Preaching morals to vicious patients seldom does any good, but you can often exert the greatest influence upon patients who indulge to excess in chewing, smoking, drinking, singing, dancing, late hours, carousing, venery, and other things that render them liable to disease. Your injunctions regarding the five things last named, if properly given, will frequently be strictly obeyed.

When drinkers tell you that they intend to " swear off " for a definite period, advise them instead of swearing off to swear neither to treat any one nor allow any one to treat them to liquor during the prescribed period. This is more manly and more apt to be observed.

The various quack bitters advertised and. guaranteed to be " a wonderful discovery," are almost invariably some vile compound of bad rum or bad whiskey, and are the origin of much drunkenness; you should point out the danger and condemn their use. If a person *will* take alcoholic stimulants, advise him to take them " barefooted "; then he will know what kind and how much he.is taking.

If you adopt the habit of presenting your photograph to every one enamored of your professional skill, or of your manners, good looks, style of dress, etc., it will be the cause of many awkward dilemmas. Many patients who would swear by you one week will curse you the next, perhaps charge that you have maltreated them, killed their children, crippled their wives, or done something else equally horrible. You will learn by melancholy experience that the minds of men (and of women too) are subject to rapid changes. Many who would regard your picture with highest esteem this month or this year, would tear it down or give it to the hangman the next. Trifles light as air will sometimes serve to detach families from you ; a whim, a caprice, a look or a nod will sometimes break links that have been forming for years ; indeed, even old patients will drop you when they get ready, with less ceremony and less regret than you would an office-boy or an hostler.

CHAPTER V.

Have respect for religion. Your profession will frequently bring you into contact with the clergymen of various denominations. Do right, and you will not only find in them firm friends, but also your chief supporters in many of your most trying cases. The ministrations of a cheerful, sensible and pious clergyman who confines himself to his true work are sometimes more useful to a worn and irritated patient than medicine; and even where death is near and inevitable, resignation often takes the place of fear and despondency when the invalid is skilfully informed of the probability of death. In fact, when cheered and fortified by religion, and impressed with the thought that whatever occurs they are in God's hands, many show as little regret upon learning that they will probably die as a traveller does when about to start on a pleasant journey.

When called to attend cases of angina pectoris, aneurism, organic heart disease, desperate wounds or injuries, apoplexy, or other diseases that create liability to sudden death, prudence may require you to conceal the danger of death from the patient, lest he at once give up all hope and be overcome by apprehension and terror; fear may exercise a deadly influence, and has often rendered mild diseases fatal. But be sure in such cases to give

[107]

private warning to those most interested. Allow no one to sink away and die without making the probability known to relatives, friends or neighbors. Be also exceedingly careful in talking before children with scarlatina, variola, rubeola, etc., of the danger of complications, or of their illness being serious or dangerous; also take care to banish from them the fear of hydrophobia, lockjaw, etc., because some very young children fully realize the meaning of death, and such talk would terrify them. Also use suitable caution in speaking within hearing of patients who seem to be sleeping, drunk, semi-comatose, etc.

It is just as natural to die as it is to be born, and every one's time must come. You can neither see what is written in the book of life, nor detain the sick soul when the Angel of Death summons; sometimes you will seem to be fighting death itself, and yet see the patient recover as if by resurrection, whilst on the other hand, you will often discover that patients are almost in the toils of death, while all around think, till you tell them differently, that they are getting better.

You should never attempt to thrust your religious beliefs, or disbeliefs, or your political tenets, upon patients who hold opposite views. It is really no part of your duty to proselyte or to administer to the religious cravings of the sick. Every sect has teachers of its own, to whom you must leave the spiritual. Confine your ministrations to the worldly welfare of patients, and never suggest anything in religious matters that involves a creed different from that of the sufferer.

The great prospect of eternity certainly overshadows

all temporal things. Be ever ready, not only to allow, but to advise patients to have spiritual comfort. Religion does good, not only hereafter, but here; indeed, the presence of religious faith is a power that can assuage the keenest sorrow and suffering, and even make the avenues to death smooth, and if any physician does not recognise it, he lacks the a b c of philosophy and the rudiments of observation. You will see many a poor, sick, woe-worn, despondent and broken-hearted wretch calmed in mind and soothed in body by its cheering influence, and aided by it to get well, if his ailments are at all curable; if not curable, his spiritual wants being supplied, he gets faith, hope, patience and resignation from it, and becomes willing, or even anxious for the hour of departure.

The automatic, seemingly anxious movements unconsciously made by the dying are popularly supposed to be attempts to communicate some remaining thoughts, or secrets, or special wish before death. Explain to the friends in such cases that Providence has kindly drawn the veil of unconsciousness around the dying one and that he is not suffering. The dying struggle is painless to the unconscious patient, but is awfully painful and harrowing to all who stand at the bedside and witness it.

It is well that you, as a physician, whether a Roman Catholic or not, should be familiar with the following duties required by Catholic patients.

When attending in Catholic families, be doubly cautious to warn the immediate friends of danger, that the sufferer may receive the last sacraments.

One of the seven sacraments of the Holy Church of Rome is Extreme Unction. It is believed to purify the soul of the dying from any sin not previously expiated through other sacraments, and to give strength and grace for the death struggle.

That church teaches that moral responsibility begins at the age of reason; therefore Extreme Unction is necessary for all who have attained that age.

Extreme Unction is given but once in the same illness, but if the patient has recovered and shortly afterward has the same, or any other kind of dangerous sickness, this sacrament is again necessary.

Another of the seven sacraments of the Church of Rome, with which you should be familiar, is the Holy Eucharist.

The Holy Eucharist, sometimes called the Wafer, is believed to contain Christ's whole being, his body, soul and divinity. It may be administered frequently in all cases of sickness where the patient is confined to the bed or to the house for any length of time, provided he has sufficient reason to make a full confession.

If the course of the disease in your patient is likely to render him unconscious, be careful to inform the family of the fact, so that the clergy may be called, and the confession be heard, and the Holy Eucharist given before the reasoning powers are obscured.

Those who are to receive the Holy Eucharist are required to fast, if possible, from midnight until they have received it; but if you consider that your patient's being without either food or medicine would be detrimental to his welfare, the clergy should be informed.

Where there is incessant nausea and vomiting, the Holy Eucharist is either not given at all, or given in the smallest quantity. To expose it to being vomited is a grave irreverence.

Be also equally careful in Catholic families to administer, or have administered, conditional baptism to all children during or after birth, when there is the slightest reason to doubt their viability. The following are the conditions and details of conditional baptism :

You, or any one else, whether a Roman Catholic or not, are allowed to administer it. A male adult is preferable to a female, and of course a Catholic, if one is at hand, to a non-Catholic. The baptism is given as follows: After procuring a glass or cup of clean water (spring water is designated, but hydrant, or pump, or any other kind of true and natural water will do), with suitable manner say, " I baptize thee in the Name of the Father," precisely at the word "Father" *pouring* a small portion of the water upon the child's head ; continue, "And of the Son," at the word " Son " *pouring* another small portion ; again continue, "And of the Holy Ghost," and at the word "Holy Ghost" another small portion.

Remember that in baptism every word must be uttered ; were you to omit even an " of," the baptism would be insufficient. Also remember that the water must be true and natural, and must be poured exactly whilst the formal words are pronounced. So very important are these details that if you arrive after a midwife or other person has baptized the child, carefully ascertain whether she has observed the full form and used accurate language. If she has not, and the danger of death continues, you should baptize it again. In such a case it is necessary to preface the formal words with : "If thou art not already baptized, I baptize thee," etc.

If in a midwifery case the child of Catholic parents is believed to be in danger of dying, it must be baptized. If it is partly born, baptize on its head, if the head is presenting ; if not, upon the hand, or foot, or any other part that is born. If no part is born, and if you can reach the child through the vagina, the water must be applied to whatever part can be touched. In all cases of unborn children, preface the regular form with the words " If thou canst be baptized, I baptize," etc. In such a case apply the water to its body with a syringe, or by any other plan that will keep the water uncontaminated till it touches the child.

You will take great risk if you use the forceps in Catholic families before the child has been baptized; for if this has been neglected and the child is born dead, you will not readily be forgiven.

Remember that it is better for a person to be prepared thrice and not go, than to go unprepared ; therefore, if you err at all, let it be on the safe side.

You should be careful to give timely notice of danger to all who have unfinished business of vital moment; persons suddenly seized may wish to summon friends, make wills, etc.

In an adult with almost any sickness you can safely predict that a hearse will be at his door in a few days, at furthest, after the pulse has gradually increased to 160.

If you will observe closely, you will find that when a patient is firmly impressed with the belief that he will die he is extremely apt to do so.

It is very much better for you to avoid leaving your sphere of physician to become a witness to wills; if called upon to do so, decline anyhow if you are not fully satisfied of the mental capacity of the testator, and never take part in interfering with the settlement, or division of the estate of those whom you have attended, as you may thereby incur the charge of abusing opportunities which you owe solely to your position as a medical attendant.

In no case be a witness to or executor of a will, when you are made a legatee or heir.

Be careful to exhibit proper gravity and sincerity when attending serious cases, and do not cry hope, hope! when you see no hope.

If a very ill, sane adult really wishes to know whether he is likely to die and asks you the plain question, answer him frankly and truthfully; but, if possible, answer him in bland terms, so as not to appall him and injure him by taking away all hope and substituting despair. With your opinion, give all the encouragement you honestly can, and if you know anything favorable, either in his physical or spiritual condition, mention it as a solace.

You are at liberty to be silent, or to say but little regarding the nature or degree of a person's sickness, but, of course, let whatever you do say, whether much or little, be true. You must not, you can not, put falsehood in the place of truth, even when solacing the sick and dying;

for, as a man and as a physician, you cannot sacrifice principle or honor for expediency, under any circumstances. But you can, you must, soften the truth and tell it in a proper manner.

You will find few who have the mental fortitude to enjoy the remainder of life, after they are formally told that their cases are permanent or incurable; and you should be cautious, not suddenly to cut off all hope, even from those afflicted with tuberculosis, cancer, Bright's disease, etc., where death approaches slowly like a creeping shadow, up to the last stage, since persons with those diseases have plenty of time, while sinking away gradually, to realize their fate. Indeed, you should not, in such cases, give a prognosis containing neither hope nor encouragement, unless you are willing to be replaced by some one, who may do no more good than you, except talking more hopefully.

You can often prevent anxious patients, whose pulse or temperature has grown worse, or those whose diseased lungs, heart, etc., you are examining, from asking you questions that would compel you to disclose to them your gloomy prognosis, by having ready on your tongue's end questions regarding their sleep, or appetite, or bowels, or something else, to ask the moment you finish listening, counting, or testing; you thus give them no chance to inquire what you find or think.

It is for several reasons better not entirely to abandon cases of consumption, cancer, etc., even though they be incurable, or in their last stages; on the contrary, keep them on your list, and visit them, at least occasionally, not only that you may give them all the relief you can, but that their friends, both present and absent, may have the very great consolation of knowing that they have full professional care and comfort.

At every period of your career aim to convince the world that your profession is not in league with death, but that on the contrary all its symbols are indicative of health-giving and life-restoring power. Neither Hygeia, nor her father, Æsculapius, is represented with the habiliments of mourning, but we see instead Æsculapius armed with serpents, the symbol of wisdom and convalescence.

Remember that Death is the physician's great antagonist, and that when he overcomes your efforts and takes away the spark of life, your duty ends. Do not, then, essay to offer up a prayer or stay and administer nervines to relatives or friends, or tender your services for promiscuous duties, e. g., carrying messages, going for the barber, undertaker, etc., but at the earliest suitable moment quietly withdraw.

Leave the laying out of the body, the application of preservative fluids to the face and body of the dead, and all such things, to the undertaker or friends.

Do not make a habit of visiting the mourning house to view the dead, and even avoid attending the funeral of dead patients, except when it is absolutely necessary.

Above all else, do not write apologetic letters to the bereaved, expressing self-reproach for not recognizing this or that fact, or regret at not following a different course of treatment, and asking forgiveness. If there are facts connected with your relations to the case that require explaining, find occasion to communicate them verbally.

Avoid all such tricks as assuring a timid patient that you will not lance his boil, but merely wish to examine it, and then suddenly doing what you assured him you would not do. Veracity should ever be your golden shield.

The white and the black, the rich and the poor, the courtezan, the outlaw, the swaggering rowdy and the reprobate, will all be represented in your practice. Attend anybody if you must, but seek to avoid disreputable places, and persons who are low down in the moral scale; they are more likely to be a curse than a blessing. Remember always that such people respect no physician who does not respect himself.

Endeavor to establish and maintain a complete professional influence over all patients you attend, for without their faith and their respect you will have to contend not only against the physical condition, but also the mental and moral.

You have a perfect right to relinquish attendance on a case when you think your interest, or your reputation, requires it; when you do so, let your withdrawal be fully understood. It is better, however, to plead having *too much other business,* and not take undesirable cases at all, than to take them and involve yourself, and afterwards relinquish or neglect them.

Never refuse to rise from bed and make night visits to patients who require them; to do so would be unjust, in that it would put your duty on some other physician, and cause the patient unnecessary suffering, perhaps death, or it might even drive the messenger to a druggist for advice and medicine, or open the door to an

Irregular, or whoever else could be caught up in the emergency, to fill your place. If, however, you charge full *night-visit* fees for *all* visits made after bedtime, you will be less often compelled to undergo loss of rest and exposure in attending those who could have sent at a more seasonable time. *Unnecessary* night-visits rob physicians of their rest, and even if they bring in fees, these are not an equivalent for the over-work and risk of health.

Be exceedingly cautious about taking patients who are to be visited clandestinely, or having married women, or young females, consult you secretly at your office; especially, if to have vaginal or other private examinations made without knowledge of parents or husband. Be careful about attending patients under pretence that they have other than the real disease in order to shield them by deceiving friends or relatives.

Do not over-visit your patients, and be especially careful to pay but few visits to those with trifling injuries, uncomplicated cases of measles, mumps, whooping-cough, chicken-pox, etc. People observe and criticise a physician's course in all such cases, and if he seems over-attentive, they are apt to believe either that they are sicker than he admits, which will cause them great alarm, or that he is *nursing* the case and creating a bill *unnecessarily*. It is sometimes an extremely delicate point to decide whether a patient needs another visit or not, and how soon. You must learn to judge correctly the proper time to cease attendance in different varieties of cases.

Most people dread the expense of medical services, and excessive attention and numerous visits are rarely appreciated; a physician who pays but few visits, and yet cures, is always popular. If you can get the reputation of not paying any but necessary visits, it will be a special feature in your favor, and will almost double your practice.

A good rule, the only proper rule, is to visit your patient when, and only when, you think he really needs your care, whether once a day, or once in seven days. Never go several times a day, without pointing out to him the necessity for it.

Above all else, avoid running in to visit patients unnecessarily because you "happen to be in the neighborhood." If you visit on such a plea and charge for it, you will be criticised and your bill may be disputed. On the other hand, never visit an ill patient so seldom, or so irregularly, as to induce a belief that you are neglectful.

Some well-to-do, or over-solicitous people form an exception to this rule, and insist on your visiting them frequently, almost living at their house during sickness, to observe progress, instruct attendants, etc., regardless of the additional expense, and, of. course, you should gratify them, but you should also at the beginning inform the person who will have to pay the bill, of the reason for the extra visits, and of the expense it entails, and get his acquiescence.

During these frequent visits you should maintain a strictly professional attitude, and avoid digressing from the patient to politics, fashions, or other current topics; unless you do so, he will certainly lose confidence, after which you will be shorn of your influence, and will scarcely be welcomed when you call.

When visiting a patient, always let it be known whether you will visit him again, and when; it will not only satisfy him, but will prevent all uncertainty. When a case has so far convalesced as to make frequent visits unnecessary, and yet mends so slowly or irregularly as to make you fear an arrest of improvement or a relapse, it is better to keep sight of it by calling once in a while, and letting it be known when you will call again, with an understanding that if the patient gets worse in the meanwhile, or if he grows so much better as to render your promised visit unnecessary, you shall be notified. This plan is, for many reasons, better than quitting such cases abruptly.

Earnestness and interest shown in cases are master qualities. They inspire faith and confidence, and are often actually accepted in lieu of extra skill. Imbue yourself with genuine interest in your cases, and you will be sure to show it in a thousand ways.

Make it a study to remember well all that is said or done at each of your visits, so that all you say and do throughout the case may be consistent. Also take care neither to expose a want of memory nor a lack of interest; were you to ask a patient "What kind of medicine did I give you last?" or hesitate in your questions, he and his friends would notice it instantly, and think you either felt but little interest in his case or had a dangerous lack of memory.

Try to make your address and manner such that patients will not hesitate to fully impart to you their secrets and the nature and seat of their disease. One of the greatest drawbacks to many physicians is that they do not inspire complete confidence, and patients neither intrust them with the secrets of their ignorance, folly, or wickedness, nor employ them in afflictions that create hesitation or shame.

Do not let your wife or any one else know your professional secrets, or the private details of your cases, even though they are not secrets; few persons like to have told from house to house what they said in their delirium, or how they shrank from leech-bites, or gagged at a pill, or to have their whims, fancies or weaknesses exposed.

Many persons believe that physicians who allow their wives to ride around with them while making visits, relate everything that has taken place at the visit after they drive away from the house. Of course this is not so, but if people think so, their discomfort is the same as though it were.

There is no end to the mortifications, compromises and estrangements a physician's prying wife may bring him into. Nothing is more mortifying or hurtful to the feelings of sensitive patients than to hear that the details of their cases are being whispered about as coming from the physician, or his wife, or others whom he or she has told.

If you allow yourself to fall into the habit of speaking too freely even of ordinary affections, or submit to be indiscriminately interviewed by chatty people concerning your patients, your very silence in disreputable cases will betray them. The credit of whole families and the character of its individual members will sometimes be at stake, and unless you shut your eyes and do not see too much, and your mouth and do not say too much, it may ruin them and involve you.

You will be allowed to see people in a very different light from that by which other people view them. The community see one another with a veil thrown over their moral and physical afflictions, over their blasted hopes, and the sorrows that flow from love and hatred; over their poverty, their frailties and their crimes, their vexations, their fears and their solicitudes; *you* will see their deformities, infirmities and deficiencies with the veil lifted, and will become the repository of all kinds of moral and physical secrets.

Love, debt or guilt may prey on the mind of a sick person and actually convert a simple into an incurable disease. As these things are apt to be kept concealed from you, it is necessary for you to be ever mindful that they are important agencies in the causation and intensification of disease, and to be prepared for their early recognition.

Observe reticence at your visits, and do not mention the private affairs of anybody from house to house. Seal your lips to the fact that patients have or ever had venereal diseases, hemorrhoids, fistula, ruptures, leucorrhœa or constipation, or that abortions, private operations, etc., have taken place, or that any person takes anodynes or liquor, or that Mrs. —— had a baby too soon after marriage, or that —— had one without being married at all, or that Mr. —— is addicted to secret immoralities, or has this, that or the other bad habit. No matter how remote the time, if patients wish their secrets told, let them do the telling. You have no right to tell the affairs of patients to any one without their consent.

But while silence should be your motto, it is your duty to society and to the state to expose and bring to justice abortionists, unprincipled quacks and heartless vampires, whether acting under cover of a diploma or not, whenever you meet with proof of their wicked work. But never charge any one with dishonorable or criminal conduct, unless you have at hand ample and positive proof of his wrong-doing; for, if you are without it, the accused is sure to make an indignant denial, and to bring against you a counter-charge of malicious persecution.

In prescribing medicines for the sick, it is better to confine yourself to a limited number of remedies with whose uses and powers you are fully acquainted, than to employ a larger number of ill-understood ones.

When you order unusually heavy doses of opiates, etc., instead of using the common signs, take care either to write the quantity out in full, or to underscore both name and quantity. It is safer also to put the names of heavy-dosed patients on their prescriptions. When you order morphia, etc., in unusually large doses, it is well to have it made into pills or granules, and direct the druggist to "put them into a bottle." It is so unusual to dispense pills in a bottle, that it informs the compounder that the quantity is not a mistake, but is as intended, and guards patients and attendants against taking, or giving them in mistake. When you prescribe pills, powders, etc., for sailors and persons whose business exposes them to get their medicines wet or wasted, it is better to direct them to be put into bottles or tin boxes instead of paper boxes.

A placebo, or tentative remedy should, as a rule, be small and easy to take. A very good form is prepared thus : Purchase a pound box of No. 35 unmedicated homœopathic globules, which cost but thirty-five cents, and immerse one half of them in fluid ext. of belladonna, and the other half in compound tinct. of iodine, for twenty minutes, then roll them about on a newspaper till all surplus fluid is absorbed, and let them dry ; after which they can be put into bottles, with a small quantity of powdered cinnamon in one bottle, and powdered liquorice root in the other, to prevent agglutination. These can either be given as globules, or put between paper, crushed, and given as powders; they make cleanly, convenient placeboes for office use, and a pound costs so near nothing, and will last so long, that you can afford to give them away and charge such patients for advice only. They will suit almost any case requiring a placebo. Be careful to keep a straight face and to give minute directions concerning the manner and time of using inert remedies given simply to amuse people who are morbid on the subject of health, and you will do them double good.

You will not only find that placeboes amuse and satisfy people, but you will often be surprised to hear that some full-of-faith placebo-takers are chanting your praise and are actually willing to swear that they were cured of one or another awful thing ‚by them; cheated into a feeling of health by globules, or teaspoonful doses of flavored water, or liquorice powder, as if by a charm. Some who seem to be magically benefited by a teaspoonful of—nothing—will actually thank you for saving their lives. What a sad comment on the discerning power of the nineteenth century! What a sad fact for legitimate medicine! What a gold mine for humbugs!

Just here let me impress a caution : to believe too much and not to believe at all, are both unfortunate mental conditions for those who practise medicine. Take care that your mind is not led into an exaggerated view of the importance and power of drugs; you must also guard against the opposite error—to which the above expressions might seem to give support—that they are useless and unnecessary; either view would materially impair, if not destroy, your fitness for the practical duties of your profession.

Never send a patient to the drug-store with a prescription for bread-pills. It is not right to make any one pay for bogus medicine; besides, if, from among all the articles in the pharmacopœia you cannot devise some trifling placebo that is more plausible than bread-pills, you must have an unusual paucity of resources. Moreover, were a patient to discover that he had been paying for such a thoroughly insipid cheat, he would naturally feel victimized and indignant.

The vast majority of people are now sensible enough to take medicine only when sickness demands it, and even then not too much. But taking a little medicine in the spring of the year with a view to " cleaning out the insides, or clearing up the constitution," and thus make the machine work better, still has a few patrons ; and cathartics and other depleting remedies are still popular with the few who cling to the old craze of *forty years ago* for purging, sweating, vomiting, etc.

These people always want to see and feel promptly and fully the action of medicines, and some of them think they could scarcely live a month unless they had almost turned themselves wrong side out with pills, salts, etc. Consequently they incline to purge themselves entirely too often. Remember that when nature is depended on, the bowels ought to act daily, or at least freely once in two or three days; for, when nature moves the bowels, the lower portion only of the intestinal cavity is evacuated, and during the interval, before the next passage, the feces from above come down and are in turn evacuated; but, when a purgative is taken, it sweeps out the entire alimentary canal, and of course such a scouring is not required as often as the natural, though partial evacuation. For any adult who cannot have an evacuation without the aid of medicine, to give a purgative once in three or four days is sufficiently often.

Never solicit people, either by word or manner, to employ you; for such a course would surely repel them, or at least prevent your enjoying the necessary esteem.

Many people are naturally fickle and capricious, and no matter how earnestly one tries to serve and satisfy them, they will quickly become wearied and disheartened, and will insist upon consultations even in the most trifling ailments; they will change about with astonishing rapidity—first from one physician to another, then to a prescribing druggist or irregular practitioner, and will finally wind up with a quack medicine, or a quack. Others, truer, will adhere to you through everything, good and bad, with surprising tenacity. You should found your hope of being retained, no matter what class of patients you are treating, upon deserving it. Do not, however, set your heart or faith upon the continuance of the patronage of any one, for you will many a time be replaced by those whom you know to be far below you in everything that goes to constitute a good physician. Sometimes you will be unexpectedly and unjustly dropped by a family, and the most ignorant or shallow fellow in the whole section, or an old lady, or an Irregular, will supersede you, and you may have to bear the reflection and the wrong without showing the slightest chagrin.

Ability promptly to detect loss of confidence, or dissatisfaction with yourself or your remedies, is one of the acquirements which, if you do not already possess, you must seek to attain. Remember that continued suffering, protracted confinement and disappointed expectation of convalescence, all tend to produce impatience and dissatisfaction in the mind of the patient and among his friends, and to create doubts of your knowledge, skill, or judgment.

A patient has a legal right to dismiss you from a case, and you have also a perfect right to relinquish attendance on him, at any time. Indeed, you may sometimes find yourself so hampered, or harassed, or maltreated in a case, that to retire from it is your only alternative.

When you find it necessary to withraw from a case, endeavor to do so in a courteous manner, as it is not incumbent on you to break off all friendly relations on this account.

Whenever dismissed from a case, consider attentively the combination of circumstances that conspired to produce the dismissal, and how you might have averted it, that you may, by self-training, gain additional familiarity with the art of doing your duty acceptably, and of retaining your patients.

Some people, indeed whole families, who will almost idolize you as long as you are lucky and have no unfortunate cases, nor deaths in their families, will turn as rudely and maliciously against you, as soon as either occur—as if you kept the book of life and controlled the hand of God.

When you are unjustifiably dismissed from a case, especially if it is to make room for an Irregular, do not consent tamely to be thrown aside in such a manner. Express your perfect willingness to retire, but make known in a gentlemanly way, that such treatment wounds your sensibilities, casts undeserved reflection on you, and injures your reputation in the community, to all of which you cannot be indifferent. Such a protest will not only enable you to vent your feelings, but will also secure for you greatly-increased respect, and will counteract the injury consequent upon your dismissal better than if you meekly submit without protesting.

In acutely painful cases, large, even heroic doses of morphia or other potent medicine are often required, and must be given promptly, as hours, or even minutes may decide the result; care must, of course, be taken that the total amount be not sufficient to poison the patient. The following case will illustrate: A gentleman known to the author, had cholera morbus; a physician was called, who prescribed for him twelve opium pills, one to be taken every six hours. In that case the physician was fatally slow in his therapeutics; for long before the time to take the second pill had arrived, the soul of that pain-racked sufferer had taken its flight to a land where medicine is not needed and six-hour intervals can do no harm. Take care to avoid his error, and never leave long intervals between the doses for patients suffering acute pain.

Bear in mind that an opiate that has power to relieve acute pain will do so within an hour; failure to do so necessitates another dose. A dose of chloral will produce sleep within half an hour, if at all, and it is useless to wait longer before repeating. When it is intended to keep a patient under the influence of opiates, it is necessary to repeat them every four hours, as the effects of a dose begin to wear off after that time.

When opiates are no longer needed, the nausea that might follow their abrupt withdrawal may be prevented by continuing them in decreased doses at four-hour intervals, decreasing the dose each time to one-half of that which preceded it.

There is a popular belief that opiates are given only to allay or relieve pain, not to cure the sickness. Opiates are not only palliatives, but by controlling pain, restlessness, etc., they are powerful curatives in a long list of diseases.

The laity expect you to examine your patient at every visit. Let your first examination be specially thorough, omit nothing that can shed light on the case, and never neglect the following five cardinal duties: To feel the pulse, to examine the tongue, to inquire about the appetite, the sleep, and the bowels. No matter what the case may be, take care to attend to these and all other evident or special duties at every visit..

Whenever symptoms render it probable that hernia, carcinoma uteri, Bright's disease, or heart disease is present; or that the throat is diphtheritic, or the ear occluded by wax, or that a tumor or an aneurism exists, or that the patient is pregnant, or that any other condition exists which, if overlooked, might imperil the patient's life and possibly make you feel the pangs of remorse for having committed a grave mistake, or subject you to disgrace if discovered by another, you should always make an immediate and thorough examination, and it would even not be out of place if you hinted gently at your suspicions.

To mistake a tumor for pregnancy, or vice versa, is one of the most mortifying and damaging of errors. To be attending a female who has been ailing for weeks or months, and who proves to be pregnant, is also very damaging unless you have recognized and declared that fact, since if you have not, her entire illness will be charged to the pregnancy. You will be lucky if you get your fees in such cases without dispute.

Never ask an unnecessary question, yet be careful to make every inquiry needed in order to learn all the facts, and to satisfy everybody that you feel an interest; if you neglect this, you will risk both error and loss of confidence.

Prompt detection of dangerous changes, or of the approach of death, not only protects the doctor, but gives him éclat if he points them out before the patient or friends observe them.

9

Never speak of anything you do for a patient as an experiment; everybody, everywhere, is opposed to physicians "trying experiments" upon themselves or theirs. For the same reason, it is not discreet to give certain patients the sample bottle of new pharmaceuticals sent to you for trial, or to let any one know that he is the *first* to whom you ever gave this or that medicine, or that his is the first case of that kind of fracture, or of smallpox, or of hernia, or of anything else that you ever attended.

You should keep a reference book for recording particularly good remedies, prescriptions for stubborn diseases, etc.; also a case book for recording the date, diagnosis, treatment, etc., of unusually important cases. Nothing impresses a patient who has a complicated or long-standing disease, with a conviction that you are interested in him, and that you intend to try your utmost to do him good, so much as to know that you keep a regular record of his case.

When truth will allow, let your diagnosis either include the patient's belief, or fully nullify it, that his mind may not distrust your opinion or antagonize your treatment.

You can more easily and permanently convince and impress a cavilling patient of a medical fact that militates against his wish or belief, for instance, that shortening is usual after fracture, by showing it to him in the books, than by a hundred verbal statements.

Study to be fertile in expedients, and never confess, or allow the inference, that you are hopelessly puzzled about a case, or have reached the limit of your resources.

Never be too sanguine of a patient's recovery from a serious affliction, and never give one up to die in acute disease, unless dissolution is actually in progress; and above all else, never withdraw from a case of acute, or self-limiting disease because the patient is very ill, and more likely to die than to live. It is highly comforting to anxious relatives or friends to know that the physician stands ready and willing to do more, if opportunity offers.

If a patient is unable to swallow, think of the œsophageal tube, or if food taken into the stomach is not assimilated, continue your efforts with inunctions of cod liver oil, or oil and quinia, rectal alimentation, etc., until he is either better, or the breath is out of his body; for *nature*, by a crisis, or a vicarious function, or a compensatory process, or the tardy action of the remedies you have used, may turn the scale and let the life-power rally and gain control over the disease at the last hour; under such circumstances, if you have given up the case as hopeless, you will be disgraced, while some brother physician, or an Irregular, or an old woman who has stepped in at the lucky moment, will reap all the glory.

CHAPTER VI.

You will have to foresee thousands of snags that lie in the professional current to catch the unwary. When in doubt whether duty requires you to do a thing or not, remember that the sin of omission is, in appearance at least, not so great as the sin of commission.

Summon professional assistance in all ugly fractures, etc., where you think there is the least danger of an unsatisfactory termination, and of your being blamed or sued in consequence, for the result. Having assistance not only divides the responsibility, but also constitutes one a teller of truth for the other, and prevents criticism and causeless suits for malpractice. Remember that the community seem to think that physicians can and must restore broken bones and injured tissues as perfectly as the Creator made them, no matter what the injury may be; and remember also that when a fracture, or dislocation, or a disfiguring wound, or accident of any kind, recovers with deformity or disability, there is danger of its serving ever after as a lasting and lingering libel on the medical attendant's reputation. Therefore the responsibility had better be divided. In this respect medical and surgical practice differ—the results of sickness usually disappear, while those of surgery remain.

Such exclamations as "Oh, no, Doctor, it cannot be that his arm (or leg) is broken, for he can work his fingers (or toes)," will often greet you when you pronounce that a bone is fractured. This error is due to the fact that people think that the fingers and toes are moved by the bones, not by the muscles. It sometimes becomes even necessary to explain this in defence of the opinion you have given.

Always take the precaution, both for the patient's protection and your own, to listen to the heart's action immediately before administering an anæsthetic; and to watch the respiration during the administration—withdrawing the agent on the least approach of blueness of the face or lips. When possible, have another physician present whenever you produce anæsthesia, more especially if the patient is a female. Also, have a third person present at all sexual examinations of females, to disprove possible hallucinations regarding either improper words or deeds and to prevent scandal.

Patients sometimes refuse to allow the physician to make examinations that require uncovering the body, or to allow him to see the underclothing, simply because they are unclean and unfit to be seen, while the physician supposes that they refuse through modesty on account of the exposure. In many such cases it is better, instead of insisting on an immediate examination, to respect their delicacy in the matter and allow an opportunity for a change of linen, etc., by appointing a time for making the examination.

Curious-minded husbands sometimes show a determination to remain in the room during vaginal examinations, or during operations necessitating exposure of their wives' persons, and you will feel tempted to ask them to retire that *they* may escape the indelicate sight, and *you* the embarrassment. If asked to retire, some might refuse to go, or do so with anger or jealousy. The better plan in such cases is to inform the husband that you are about to begin what your duty requires you to do, and he will probably retire of his own accord, unless specially requested to remain.

Expertness in detecting and contravening the various kinds of scandal and calumny admits of cultivation to a great degree; so also does ability to foresee and escape entanglement with the captious, the bad, silly tattlers, the fraudulent, etc.

Jealous midwives, ignorant doctor-women, and busy neighbors often exert a malign influence, and tell tales or circulate falsehoods about physicians that must be noticed and thwarted according to the necessities of the case.

Tact and nice discernment in establishing and maintaining a proper attitude toward nurses and other attendants on the sick is a valuable gift that will prevent or counteract possible machinations. To give attendants credit on proper occasions for faithfulness is not only just and gratifying to them, but makes firm friends of them; moreover, such public endorsement encourages them to do their best to maintain the reputation which you have given them.

A bad nurse may render a curable case fatal by improperly indulging the patient's appetite for food or drink; or by neglecting to give him medicine, drink, diet, etc., at the proper time, or in the manner directed; or by appropriating his food or robbing him of the liquors you suppose he takes; or by keeping him too hot, or too cold, or giving him too much, or too little fresh air; or by getting drunk or becoming careless, etc., etc.

The conciliation of anxious, captious, impatient or dissatisfied friends of the sick, when sickness is not progressing satisfactorily, naturally requires great skill and a profound study of human nature.

Scandal-mongers and malicious liars will often lie in ambush for you, and must be met or checkmated by the most available means ; to judge what is best to be done under the circumstances is sometimes a most annoying and puzzling question.

In serious or strange cases, and in such as engender great public excitement, if you indulge in confidential or semi-confidential whispers to the rabble, or give out daily bulletins to them, it will often give rise to misrepresentation, or even to total perversion of what you really did say or mean, and your statements may come back to you so changed as to require tedious explanations from you. Be ever on the alert for this danger. If necessary, give your opinion to the proper persons in writing, to prevent its being misconstrued or misquoted.

When a sick person puts himself under your care he gives you a responsible duty to perform. If he then neglects or refuses to take your remedies, or obeys your instructions in an imperfect manner, he ties your hands and frustrates your efforts for his relief, and cannot hold you to full responsibility in the case. If, however, he will not or cannot do exactly as you wish, and if no special danger exists, it is sometimes better, after drawing attention to the position in which you are placed (as a protection to yourself), to humor his whims or childish weaknesses, and modify or alter your therapeutics so as to meet his wishes and ability. This you can do good-naturedly, without fully yielding to him or compromising your authority or your dignity. The wishes, prejudices and errors of peculiar patients must be studied and to a certain extent respected. To do this is a matter of policy, and is very different from yielding a question of principle.

Never captiously oppose a remedy because it is suggested by a layman. The most ignorant person may make a wise suggestion ; and laymen often talk excellent sense about facts which have come to their notice. Listen patiently to all sensible propositions, and if they seem simple and meritorious you may find it well to add them to your other means, for their moral effect, if nothing more. Be frank in giving credit to any good idea, no matter by whom advanced. When rejecting a remedy thus tendered, let it be known that your condemnation arises from conviction, and not from superciliousness. You may in some cases even humor a whim and sanction the use of harmless domestic remedies,— saffron tea, plasters, onions to the feet, etc., in conjunction with your more reliable agents.

Make it a rule to accord persons credit for well-meant deeds, even though they may be valueless in themselves; also, when possible, to approve domestic treatment employed before you were sent for; at least do not condemn it in a violent or offensive manner. Listen patiently to those around while they relate how they did the best they knew, and do not pooh-pooh, shrug your shoulders, or smile sarcastically, and thus belittle their honest efforts to relieve the sufferer.

Your cordial approval of their simples, used in good faith with true and loving motives, will redound greatly to your credit, and greatly enhance your reputation for kindness and sympathy.

When attending certain classes of very ill patients, e. g., the wife of a druggist or the child of a physician, if there is any simple remedy in which they have great faith and which they wish to try, every consideration should incline you, unless there is some clear contra-indication, to acquiesce and allow it, in conjunction with your other means.

It will be a trying ordeal when you, by accident, meet an " old lady who has an infallible salve," good for anything from mosquito bites up to elephantiasis. You will find her so full of faith in herself and in her salve that neither reason nor ridicule can shake it. Be fair and reasonable with her ; but if you indiscreetly concede to her remedy any recognition beyond its actual merits, or take her into confidence or semi-partnership in the treatment of bone felons, ulcers, wounds, etc., you will make a big mistake, and fill her as full of conceit, and of mischief, too, as the sea is of water.

Hypochondriacs, the hysterical, the mildly insane, and various other kinds of bores, will sometimes come to your office and tax your patience and ingenuity with annoying or unnecessary questions, or exaggerated descriptions of their ailments, or the details of their business, or the history of their family affairs, when you have no time to waste and yet are indisposed to be rude, till you actually wish you could fly out at the window and get away from them.

Some of these you will have to freeze out by chilling coldness in their reception. If you tell them as they come in that time is very precious with you, they cannot deem you uncivil, and will be brief, unless unusually pachydermatous. If you are greatly annoyed, keep a placard posted with " *This is my busy day.*"

When you are to be a witness in a grave court case, politely but firmly refuse to give the opposing counsel, or any other person, either a verbal or written statement of what you saw, heard or observed in the case, or what your opinion is, or what your testimony will be; also dispute their right to question you at all on the subject.

If you are yielding in this respect, you may actually aid them to set traps for you by distorting your statement from its proper meaning, or to rebut it on the witness-stand, or to charge that you are lacking in medical knowledge; thus bringing both justice and yourself to grief. Firmly but courteously inform them that you cannot give the desired information, but that they can find out all you know on the witness-stand.

When in court, whether as plaintiff, defendant, or witness, keep cool and self-possessed; guess at nothing and express no opinion for which you cannot give the why and wherefore.

There is no creed, or class, except ours, whose members habitually confute and confront one another in courts and before the public. Our so-called psychological experts, specialists and other would-be highly scientific representatives, have been hired by contestants to exhibit their power to weave favorable testimony, so often of late, in criminal cases, will cases, life insurance cases, etc., that the public jest about us, and believe from our kaleidoscopic contradictions that our boasted science of medicine is a tissue of mere guesswork. These remarks only apply to the pseudo-experts, who are willing to sell their testimony to the highest bidder.

To rid yourself of undesirable would-be patients will be one of the most difficult dilemmas that will confront you. If you are " *Too busy to attend*," it is probably the most unassailable of all excuses you can employ in these cases. To assume charge of a sick person and afterwards neglect him, is a great wrong.

When you receive calls to cases that from any cause you cannot or will not attend, notify them to get some one else, in order that the patient may be saved from delay, and you from the annoyance of repeated messages and solicitations.

No one can blame you for not being at home when you are needed; but if you are at home, and quibble or refuse to respond to a call, you will sometimes be severely criticized, especially if the case goes wrong in consequence of your not responding.

The chief objection to recommending persons you wish to cast off, to physicians whom you wish to aid, is that they are then quite sure still to hanker for you, and to involve you as a consultant or assistant to your protégé if things get serious ; whereas, if, instead of re-commending them to any particular one, you compel them to choose some one for themselves, you will get rid of them permanently.

You will occasionally encounter patients, or their wiseacre friends, who will challenge you to controversy, and presume to discuss your diagnosis and your remedies with you. Most of these are as full of doubts, beliefs and theories, as a lemon is of acid,—foreknowing and prejudging all you do, frequently thwarting your every effort,—possibly drawing the curtain aside after you go, and exposing to everybody things that should properly remain your professional secrets. If you write a pre-scription for gonorrhœa, or cough, or almost any other ailment, many a presumptuous patient, or his friend, will read it to you and actually comment, or offer to argue on it. You will be often harassed by such meddlers, and compelled to resort to various expedients to satisfy or foil them, and avoid collision with their whims and prejudices. In fact, from this cause, the good effects of mystery, hope, expectation and will-power are of late almost entirely lost to regular physicians, all special con-fidence is sapped, and all you can expect in many cases is the gross physiological action of your medicines—and prejudice and fear actually do much to thwart even that. Such meddlers will often aid in making curable diseases fatal.

The presence of self-important sick-room critics, with jealous eyes and unbridled tongues, will, if you are at all timid, often impair or destroy your usefulness, by either diverting your mind from your case, or lessening your concentration, and may even lead to mistakes in diagnosis or treatment. Consciousness of being watched, or under unfriendly criticism, will, in many cases, embarrass you, to some extent cloud your judgment, and, of course, lessen your usefulness.

It is better to leave your directions about medicine, food, etc., with the nurse, or whoever is in charge, than with the patient.

School yourself till you can prevent your thoughts and opinions from showing in your countenance, and above all, discipline your features and manner, so that nervous and ill patients cannot detect in you unfavorable reflections about themselves, which you wish to conceal.

Never prescribe large quantities; it is far better to have the prescriptions repeated over and over again, than to risk having half a bottle set aside untaken. One of the nicest little points in medical practice is to decide how large a quantity of medicine to order at a time. In many cases, it is wiser to order only sufficient medicine to last from one visit to the next.

To set aside unused medicines and order others, in such a way as not to impair confidence, requires a great deal of clever management. In many cases, where a remedy is ceasing to be useful, or indications for something different are appearing, it is better not to stop the old abruptly, as though it were wrong or doing harm, but instead, to instruct them to set it aside and begin the new at —— o'clock.

Patients will rarely complain of the price of medicines that are taken, but they will observe the waste, and criticize you, when you set one remedy aside and order others. A good plan is to order the empty bottle in which one medicine was gotten, to be washed and carried to get the next in. A medicine that has been put aside is very rarely again indicated. When you set one remedy aside, to give another, if there is a prospect of its being used again further on in the case, be sure to mention the fact. It does not then look so much like extravagance, or misjudgment in prescribing.

Be also guarded against ordering patients to buy expensive instruments, reclining chairs, supporters, braces, atomizers, or other costly articles, unless you are very sure they will answer the purpose and will be used. It is no credit to the physician to have people exhibiting this or that article which cost —— dollars, ordered by him, but for one reason or another never used, and now referred to as a shameful instance of extravagance.

You will occasionally encounter patients who have been kept in a furnace of anxiety and terror for months or years (hell on earth), through the deception of some rapacious and shameless quack, or the ignorance of some novice in the profession, who has pronounced them syphilitic, when in fact they have really never had even a sign or a symptom of that disease.

It is torment enough for those who really have constitutional syphilis, to go through life filled with remorse for the past and fear for the future, without adding spurious cases. When examination proves that the case before you is not syphilis, it is your highest duty to give such explanation and assurance as will fully banish the error from your patient's mind.

You will be sure to produce unnecessary alarm and distress in the minds of those whose chests you examine, if you tell them of "a slight deposit in the apex," "an abnormal resonance," a "bruit de diable," "râles," "a palpitation," "a disordered rhythm," or other, to them, ominous symptom. Take care never to say or do anything which will unnecessarily fix the mind of a patient on the character of his breathing, the action of his heart, etc.

You will occasionally meet persons who have been told by physicians years ago that their lungs were gone and that they would not live a year, or that they had this or that affliction which would destroy them in less than such a time. Such unnecessary forebodings cast discredit on the profession, and should draw upon those who make them the severest censure.

God only knows how many young women in our land are now tormented with apparitions of "womb complaint," which have no existence except in some physician's imagination—young women who, had the subject not been suggested to their minds, would have lived a lifetime without even a thought of such a thing as a womb.

The chief reason why there are so many spurious cases of womb disease is obvious. When a man is told he has a luxated shoulder, or a cataract, or a hernia, or a cancer, he finds many ways to confirm or refute the physician's opinion, and he can also see what the treatment is doing for him; but when a miserable woman, morbid on the mysterious subject of "womb disease," "gets examined," and is told, whether correctly or incorrectly, that her womb (like her nose) "is turned a little to one side," or "is down," "ulcerated" or "affected," it tallies exactly with her fears; and, shrinking from both the expense and the exposure to be endured, if she were to consult another doctor, she naturally submits to the manipulations and to the monetary exactions of whoever has made that examination—possibly recovering from morbid states that never existed, and paying for cures never performed. If there is a wretch meaner than all others in the sight of God, it must be the physician who, void of moral sense, would exaggerate the nature of a case and terrify the sick simply for dollars and cents.

It is also cruel to tell patients indefinitely that their trouble comes from their heart, or kidneys, or liver, or lungs, or that they have the "liver complaint" or "kidney disease," or that their lungs are "affected," when there is only some slight or temporary affection of these organs. And it is still more cruel and unwise to predict immediate or impending death, even if you discover serious organic disease of lung or heart. The duration of life will depend on many circumstances that you cannot always foresee; the carefulness and prudence of the patient, the conservative powers of the system, the compensative efforts of nature, etc. You know that a man's liver or his lungs or his heart may be deranged this week and well next; but many people think that if any of these organs are affected in any way it is necessarily permanent, and it gives them constant anxiety. Many people are at this moment living in as great anxiety as though a sword were suspended over them by a hair, because they were told long ago that such and such an organ was affected, without explanation being given of the functional or temporary character of the derangement. Contrary to the belief of the laity, and of some physicians, sudden death rarely occurs in heart disease, except in aortic obstruction and regurgitation. By explaining the difference between temporary ailments and those of a permanent character, or the difference between a functional and an organic affection, you will avoid magnifying real ailments or creating imaginary ones, and give many a patient perpetual sunshine in exchange for constant gloom. It is your duty at least to avoid all ambiguity of language in such cases.

In nervous, hysterical and impressible persons, it is possible to convert a slight, or even imaginary complaint, or functional trouble into a serious one by fixing their attention on the organ deranged; hence, in these cases, ignorance is bliss, and the physician should divert the mind of the patient as much as possible from the real or supposed seat of disease, even if he has to treat it unconsciously to the patient.

Even our instruments of precision can be used in such a manner as to become objects of dread and terror. That excellent instrument, the clinical thermometer, often tells from day to day the unwelcome truth that fever continues, till the patient and those around almost wish it had never been invented. Try to prevent, if possible, such results of its use.

Be especially careful not to allow patients' attention to be fixed on their urine. Some persons have a morbid tendency to watch this excretion, and only need a dis-

10

couraging word from a physician to make them as anxious about their kidneys—apparitions of Bright's disease, diabetes, gravel, etc., arising before their distempered vision—as some women are about their wombs.

You will also have patients lacking in the salt of wisdom, who come tormented with evil forebodings over conditions that are either imaginary or perfectly natural : some because they have discovered that their left testicle hangs lower than the right, or because their scrotum remains contracted or relaxed; others terribly alarmed because they have in examining themselves discovered the little odoriferous glands on the posterior part of their glans penis and imagine them to be chancres or cancers ; others because either fear of disease, blackmail, bastardy, or moral accusation has thwarted their attempts to copulate with loose women and led them to imagine themselves impotent. You will also occasionally be asked for advice by those about to marry, and by others newly married, who are miserable on account of this or that affliction, defect or fear. Remember in all such cases that your opinions are your capital, and charge your *full fee*, even though you write no prescription. With them the charge is for banishing fears and anxieties, and giving valuable information and satisfaction.

Be careful to warn all such people against the curse of falling into the hands of quacks, or other "friends of erring youth," through pamphlets on the evils of spermatorrhea, masturbation, etc., and tell them of the mischief such people inflict on their victim's health, and also of their unscrupulous, never-ceasing voracity for money.

It is doubtful whether the various medical guide books for the people, " Dr. Alpha's Family Medical Guide," Professor Omega's " Every one His Own Physician," and the hosts of others, do any one much good, while it is certain that they do a great deal of harm, by filling people with imaginary wisdom, and emboldening them to try their hands at doctoring cases that require a physician, till either great suffering or permanent injury is entailed, or probably life itself sacrificed.

Is it not possible that Pope had such works in view when he said :

" A little learning is a dangerous thing " ?

The eight or ten very large papillæ seen upon the base of every one's tongue, often occasion great anxiety upon being discovered by over-anxious laymen, while looking into their throats for syphilis, diphtheria, or ulcers. Great relief is expressed when they are told that these are natural.

You will be often consulted by true syphilitics, who wish to know what would be the result of their marriage. Never promise certain immunity against future outbreaks ; and do not sanction marriage, unless it has been at least three years since they contracted syphilis, and at least two years since they had any evidences of the disease. They should even then marry only under hygienic and therapeutic restrictions.

When a patient, alarmed about his health, consults you, if you want fully to satisfy him by your opinion, *be earnest*, and let attention to his case overshadow all you say or do ; above all, do not divert his conversation from himself to extraneous subjects. If it be at your office, do not digress by showing him the toy steamboat you are making, or by telling him the latest news, or the history of the cigar you are smoking, or of the newspaper you are reading, or of the cane you are twirling. If *he* diverts the conversation from his case, bring him back to it at the first opportunity.

Never recommend sexual intercourse as a remedy for self-pollution, nocturnal emissions, spermatorrhœa, hypochondriasis, acne, or anything else. If those subject to these affections choose to run the risk of syphilis, gonorrhœa, bastardy, or exposure, or to commit rape, adultery, or self-pollution, let it be on their own responsibility, not on yours. Perfect chastity is entirely compatible with good health; and I know of no disorder, either of body or mind, in which fornication is necessary.

Remember that night emissions recurring occasionally in young men, partake of the nature of an overflow, and are perfectly compatible with health. Young men, almost crazy with dread and remorse, will often consult you about these emissions. You will find that almost every one attributes them to self-pollution in boyhood. The results of self-pollution are, as a rule, not half as destructive as commonly supposed; when the habit is stopped, its results are usually quickly recovered from.

Consumptive females whose bloodmaking power is destroyed by their disease, naturally cease to menstruate. They then attribute their decline to absence of the menses, while in reality the absence of the menses is due to the decline and consequent loss of bloodmaking power. When such patients appeal to you to restore their menses, you must explain why they have ceased, and that they will not menstruate again, till their health and bloodmaking power improve.

Consumptives sometimes have hectic fever so regularly at a certain hour, day after day, that they and their friends are persuaded that their sickness is malarial in character, and if you are not on the alert, they may mislead you into giving an erroneous opinion to that effect. If quinia does no specific good for the daily fever of a weakly or broken-down person, you should suspect that it may be hectic, rather than malarial fever.

The popular belief that one is *booked* for consumption because a parent, or brother, or sister died of it, is true only in a limited sense. If the relative's disease was part of his law of development and was in his charter of life, it should indeed excite serious fears in every one who has the same charter, the same constitutional bias. But if his disease began after his physical development was fully completed, or from an accidental cause, the law of heredity does not apply. One whose father, mother, sister or brother died from phthisis, the sequence of bad hygiene, pneumonia, etc., is not thereby compromised, as that variety is not hereditary unless his father had it at the time when he begot him, or his mother had it during pregnancy or nursing.

One person in every seven firmly believes that he has either heart disease or consumption, while those really affected with either, are rarely willing to admit it; the consumptive generally to the last calling it a bad cold. You will find that the management of those who really have either is one of the most delicate questions in practice. When your opinion is invoked in these cases, do not examine or question them at all, unless you have time to do so thoroughly, for your opinion and treatment may influence their entire future course, and if anything is overlooked, you may induce a neglect of proper remedies till the patient is beyond their reach.

No wonder the mind dreads consumption, for it is humanity's great destroyer. It scourges the young, the beautiful, the gentle and the gifted, and this portion of every community is selected for its most intractable and fatal forms. ·

Valetudinarians almost invariably dress too warmly, and in their anxiety to protect their bodies from cold, they wear so much clothing that they shut all the sunlight, electric and other health-giving influences from their bodies, overheat their skin, and keep it constantly relaxed, and, of course, reduce or destroy their natural resisting power, so that when they go into cold air, or into a draft, the result is like jumping from the climate of Cuba into that of Canada. No person, sick or well, should ever wear more clothes than are sufficient to keep him comfortable. Every ounce beyond that, is unnecessary and enervating.

People of the opposite extreme, knowing that cool bedrooms are healthy for hearty well people, often carry catarrhal and croupy children and other invalids from the warm rooms, where they have passed the day, to cold sleeping-rooms, instead of giving them uniform warm air, day and night, till recovery takes place. It would even be less hurtful to reverse it and keep them in a cold room while awake, and in a warm one during sleep, because a person has more resisting power while awake, than during sleep. The butcher can attend at his exposed, fireless stall, the coldest winter weather till midnight, and not even sneeze, but were he to lie down on his stall and sleep during a similar period, he would probably get chilled and contract catarrhal pneumonia or rheumatism. It devolves on you to point out these and kindred dangers to patients, who are risking them.

Register-heat, on account of its parching dryness, is bad for both sleeping and sitting-rooms. You will often smile at seeing a small pan or cup of water simmering under a register that is pouring out a volume of over-dry, impure air, while the inmates are blissfully believing it is tempering and rendering pure and moist all the air passing over it. A very large wet towel or folded sheet hung before the opening is much more effective.

Many new-born children are unwittingly exposed to the bad effects of cold from lack of knowledge on the part of those in charge. The popular belief is that if the nurse puts plenty of clothes on a babe she has done all that is needed; whereas, if the little babe—whose heat-generating power is naturally very feeble—is put into clothes in a cold condition, without further attention, hours or days may elapse before its feeble heat-making power can bring on a reaction and warm it. Ice is put into woollen cloths or blankets to prevent it from melting; cold bread wrapped in a blanket would never warm itself, but if warmed and then wrapped in a blanket it would retain its heat for some time. Take care that the new-born babe is kept warm. As soon as it is dressed it should be nestled against its mother's bosom till warm;

if this does not suffice, it should be kept near the fire till the coldness is banished.

Remember that the act of nursing not only supplies the babe with nourishment, but also communicates the mother's heat, and possibly electricity, or some other occult, but useful influence; at any rate, it can do no harm to have all *hand-fed babes* nestled to some one's warm, bare breast at intervals of a few hours, in exact imitation of those that suck.

The ancient custom of clothing infants in flannel, with woollen socks during hot weather, creates discomfort and invites sickness. Its harmfulness should be made known to such as you find following it.

There is a widespread popular error, partaken of to some extent even by physicians, regarding the object of lancing children's gums. When a physician lances or rubs a child's swollen gums, he does so, not solely to let the tooth through, nor does he expect it instantly to pop through the opening, but his chief object is to sever the innumerable small nerves that ramify through the gum, and thus relieve the tension, irritation, danger of convulsions, etc. No one should incise or rub through a child's gums, except when these evils are present.

There exists so much prejudice on this subject among certain people, that if you lance their sick child's gums and he dies despite of it, you will risk being damned by them for doing it.

There is much less popular opposition to rubbing children's teeth through with a thimble, spoon-handle, or any other suitable article, than there is to lancing them; and the contused wound made by rubbing is less apt to reunite than a clean incision.

"Doctor, my child gets the phlegm up, but instead of spitting it out he swallows it again," is a stereotyped expression. If he does, it makes but little difference, as he swallows it, not back into the windpipe or lungs, but into the stomach, where it becomes unimportant. Of course it is unnatural for a child to spit out before it is over three years of age.

It is a popular belief that crossness in sick children argues favorably, and there often seems to be a great deal of truth in it, as it requires considerable strength and energy to exhibit crossness. At any rate the reappearance of tears in the child's eyes when crying is a favorable sign.

Never make fun of mothers because they believe their children have worms, for in some instances they are correct in their opinions, and if you scout the idea and fail to give a trial remedy, you may. be chagrined to learn that after they left you, they went to some drug-store, purchased a quack vermifuge, and sure enough brought away worms, and are exultingly telling it as proof that you were wrong and they were right. Such. cases do one's reputation no good. It is better, when worms are suspected, to give some harmless vermifuge, even though it do no other good than to test the fact and satisfy the mother.

It is better in every kind of case to allow a certain degree of weight to the opinions of the patient and his attendants, especially those who sit up with him at night; not that you should surrender your judgment for their exaggerated apprehensions or palpable errors, but, at least, listen to what they say, and consider their opinion in making up your own. The apparently cause-less fears and predictions of nurses and friends are some-times surprisingly confirmed, and the self-sufficient physician's prophecies correspondingly unrealized.

Condemn the keeping of commodes in bed rooms, as they are a dangerous source of diphtheria, typhoid fever and other filth diseases.

Every worthy housewife courts the reputation of keeping a clean house, and one of the proofs of her skill is the absence of bed-bugs, pediculi, roaches and other vermin from the premises. If you ever notice such things about a respectable patient's body, clothing or bed-room, affect not to see them, as nothing is more deeply mortifying than to have anything of the kind noticed and pointed out by the physician.

The terms scarlatina and scarlet rash are now in every-body's mouth, and are spoken of by the laity as harm-less affections, under the belief that scarlatina is a slight affection, bearing about the same relation to scarlet fever that varioloid bears to variola. There is no such dis-ease as scarlet rash, and the cases to which these terms are applied, are usually either scarlet fever or rötheln (German measles), and unless people are made to under-stand this, neglect and great damage may ensue.

Bringing out the eruption is one of nature's processes in measles, scarlatina, small-pox, etc., but there is no doubt that the large quantities of saffron tea, ginger toddy, hot lemonade, etc., used by grannies to bring them out, do more harm than good, by disordering the stomach, inflaming the eruption, etc. This "bringing out the eruption," when uncomplicated, had better be left somewhat to nature; when it is complicated, something more reliable than teas is indicated.

There is also a popular belief that all skin diseases result from humors in the blood that must be driven out, or, if already out, kept out, till killed by blood medicine, much the same as one would drive rats from their haunts and keep them out till annihilated. No patient will object to your driving his humor out, or killing it, but if he thinks you have simply driven it in, woe to you if he should afterward have any severe or fatal sickness. In such cases it is well to give an internal remedy, whether local treatment is used or not. In some cases where great fear or strong prejudice exhibits itself, it is even better to commence the internal treatment eight or ten days before beginning the local.

There is also a popular expectation of evil and a popular readiness to blame the physician if any new symptom appear after he suddenly arrests or cures diarrhœas, periodical bleedings, foot-sweat, or chronic discharges of any sort, etc.

Many persons suppose boils and various eruptions to be healthy. Even if they are, most people will agree that some other mode of health is decidedly preferable. This belief is probably founded on the fact that during convalescence after certain serious diseases a crop of boils often appears, seemingly from a revival of the energies, or vital forces of the system, from the depressing influence of the disease. The fact of their coming being coincident with reorganization and returning health, probably accounts for the belief that boils and health naturally go together

The high color of the urine occasioned by activity of the skin in patients whose sickness compels them to lie in warm beds or to keep in warm rooms, also seen in well people who perspire freely during warm weather, frequently causes alarm and induces groundless fear that they have kidney disease. Explain to them how the functions of the skin and kidneys are related, and that it makes but little difference whether the urine is scanty or abundant if it contains all the natural excreta and is simply deficient in water.

When a coin, or other small foreign body is accidentally swallowed, some old lady is almost sure to give a dose of castor oil, thus liquefying the contents of the bowels and compelling the intruder to travel the entire length of the alimentary canal alone, instead of allowing the fecal matter to remain as a mass to include it and prevent its edges and corners from doing harm. When such an article is swallowed, do not interfere with nature's efforts unless you are sure she cannot expel it unaided.

When a person faints, those around run to assist him and instinctively raise his head, instead of lowering it as they should do, thus prolonging the syncope and endangering life.

In all cases where great debility and pallor are present, be careful to instruct the attendants to keep the patient's head low, and to prevent him from rising suddenly for any purpose, and from sitting up too long, for fear of fatal syncope.

"If the dog that bites a person goes mad, the one bitten will also," has caused may a valuable dog to be killed. The truth is, if the dog's mouth or teeth contain hydrophobic virus at the time of biting the person, there is great risk of its being communicated; if not, there is no risk. If the dog is killed under the mere suspicion of having hydrophobia, the disproof of the disease is made impossible, and the person bitten and his friends are left to all the terrors of uncertainty.

Foolish persons will occasionally tell you, in a boasting manner, that they have no fear of contagious diseases, and will show by either word or manner, that they entertain the belief that contagious diseases attack those who dread them and spare those who do not. It is proper to teach such people that the laws of smallpox, syphilis, gonorrhœa, hydrophobia, typhus fever, and such affections, are very different from what they imagine; that fear cannot give them to cowards, women, or children, who stay outside of their influence, and that lack of fear will not, cannot, protect nurses, friends, old people, babes, or braggarts, if exposed to them.

There exists a popular prejudice against damp houses, leaky roofs, night air, etc., which is probably carried entirely too far. Dampness is, of course, inimical to health when mould, absence of fresh air and light, filth, or other unfavorable, disease-producing elements are added to it; but neither life on board of vessels, nor the presence of excessive dampness, as in rainy weather, is in itself unhealthful.

The low-spirited and morbid will often refer to the fulness or emptiness of the veins on the back of their hands as evidence that their blood is drying up, or that they need bleeding, or that they have consumption. Explain to them the entire lack of value of such conclusions.

As purgatives after confinement, many physicians order simples, castor oil, seidlitz powders, etc., instead of writing regular prescriptions; it will be wise for you to follow the same rule and give a lying-in woman castor oil, or whatever other simple laxative she, or her friends, are accustomed to take. If you give a lying-in woman a Latinized prescription for a purgative, and as a coincidence, she has hyper-purgation, or puerperal fever, or hemorrhages, or if syncope, or anything else follows, she will be apt to believe firmly that your mysterious purgative caused her sickness; and if she happen to die, you will be *blessed*.

Admitting or excluding those who wish to visit the sick, and allowing, or forbidding conversation with patients or within their hearing, require great delicacy and tact. Try to so manage the matter as to engender no personal enmities. Also endeavor to acquire expertness in answering anxious questions about such cases. Never attempt to exclude the parents, near relatives, or religious advisers from the room of a very ill person, except for the most urgent and obvious reasons, or you may raise among them a very natural whirlwind of indignation against you.

Never ask the age of a patient oftener than once during attendance on his case. Also take care neither to ask any question twice at the same visit, nor to do anything else that would indicate abstraction, lack of memory, or incompetence.

You will find that you will inspire more faith in a prescription if you begin to write it with an air of decision immediately after receiving, to some important question, an answer which your manner shows is what you expected.

Take care to ask all necessary questions before beginning to write your prescriptions, lest the patient think you have not included the additional information in forming your conclusion, or considered it in writing the prescription, or that your treatment was determined on before getting all the facts. Also make it a rule to ask nothing further after prescribing.

It is well to terminate your visit as soon after prescribing, as can be properly done.

CHAPTER VII.

"The successful man is the man who knows human nature, as well as his profession."—FOTHERGILL.

Every minute spent in studying how to make your remedies agreeable will be more profitable to you, than half an hour of any other kind of study. Whoever now gives much crude or coarse medicine in ordinary cases, injures both himself and his profession, and lacks one of the simplest requirements of success. Indeed, one of the greatest drawbacks to young physicians, and one of the chief reasons why they do not assist their older brethren more in superseding pleasant quackery, is that having their attention riveted on their cases, and studying more about getting them *safely* than *comfortably* through diseases, and being anxious to get the specific physiological effects of medicines quickly and fully, they too often give them in crude forms, forgetting that the majority of sick people are fastidious, and have likes and dislikes that must be respected.

A great and almost universal mistake that *regular* physicians make, is to think that when people send for physicians, they send solely to have medicines given. Many people are much more anxious to get an opinion of the nature and tendency of their case and words of assurance from the physician, than to begin a regular course of attendance and medicine.

Make special endeavors to retain every medicine-hater that falls into your hands. Such *incorrigibles* had better be under your care, with rational supervision and small doses of good treatment, than to be paying somebody else for harmful quackery or fancy nonsense.

Keep ever in your mind, that many people seem to be two-thirds spiritual and one-third animal, and that others seem to be but one-third spiritual and two-thirds animal, between which are all intermediate grades. If you attempt to treat all these alike, you will certainly fail. The mental management of the sick is often much more difficult than the physical. A close study of the mental forces and of mental therapeutics is one of the necessities that the regular profession is still extremely deficient in. Irregulars often give a mere placebo, or useless agent, which unquestioning faith (psychological energy) on the part of the patient *potentizes*, and a wonderful cure (?) results.

This is probably the most rational explanation of the fact, that newly discovered therapeutical agents, as bromide of potassium, salicylic acid, etc., make so many more wonderful cures when first heralded as remedies, than they do after they have taken a fixed rank in the pharmacopœia.

Novel remedies often assist the cure through mental influences. Many regular physicians give valuable, true remedies, but give them just as they would administer to a horse or a sheep, as if their only duty consisted in telling the sick what drugs to swallow; they seem to despise the aid of faith, hope, mystery and expectation. You must learn, in simple cases, to depend

11

more upon the aid of hygiene, diet, and mental influences, and less on large doses of medicine, which might allow room for some of your patients to say you had almost killed them.

Remember particularly, that Drs. Diet, Quiet, Hope and Faith are four excellent assistants, whose aid you should constantly invoke. Dr. Time is also in some cases very successful, but he is slow and unreliable, and unless Dr. Helpwell is called to assist, occasionally permits a curable patient to sink into his coffin, instead of restoring him.

If you indicate to a patient for whom you prescribe an unpalatable medicine, at the time when you order it, that it will have a bitterish or a saltish taste, or any other unpleasant quality, his mind will be prepared for it beforehand, and it will not seem so repulsive to him, as if his mind and palate were taken by surprise.

If the directions on the bottle indicate what a remedy is for,—for instance, if you have it labelled " apply to the injured foot as directed," or " for the pain in the chest," or " for the cough,"—it will be more apt to give a certain class of patients faith in its being a direct and proper remedy, and cause their minds to go with it, rather than against it.

Remember that even a highly proper remedy may be pushed too far, or continued too long. Indeed, cases sometimes reach a point at which it is better to stop all medicine temporarily, and depend on hygiene, diet, stimulants, nursing, etc.

Keep yourself familiar with the bad effects that may follow the use of the drugs which you administer, that you may either avoid producing them, or promptly recognize and remedy them when they occur.

Avoid as far as possible the use of medicine that must be taken " through a tube," that must be kept "in a cool place " or "in a dark place "; on which " no water must be taken "; that must be handled with caution, or that must be stopped when the eyelids begin to swell, or when the muscles begin to jerk, or that the druggist must label " Poison," especially with doubters and medicine-haters.

Some people will not send for you till they are truly ill, for fear you will put them to bed, or salivate them, or bring them misery instead of relief. Others will be afraid you will give them quinine, or injure their teeth with iron, calomel, etc., or that if they begin to take medicine they will not be able to stop. Disarm all such people by the assurance that their fears are exaggerated or groundless.

" Iron injures the teeth " is a cry which you will often hear, and it originates in the fact that muriated tincture of iron, which contains muriatic acid, if given without proper caution, will injure the teeth, not on account of the iron, however, but of the acid that is associated with it ; just as the water that makes a pot of boiling coffee would scald a person all the same if the coffee were not in it. Preparations of iron containing no free acid do not act upon the teeth.

It is popularly believed that *quinine* gets into the bones, destroys sight and hearing, causes dropsy, etc. So firmly do some people believe these things that you will have to humor their prejudices, and give them sulphate of cinchonia, compound tincture, or some other preparation of bark, when bark is indicated.

This prejudice probably depends chiefly on the fact that, being powerful for good, people naturally infer that it must be very strong and powerful for evil. It is also often due to the teachings of Irregulars, who seek through it to prejudice the public against regular physicians, while constantly but secretly using it themselves. I have known a conspicuous Irregular to denounce quinine strongly, and yet use two-grain sugar-coated quinine pills under the name of "*Panama Beans*" for the cure of his patient. We know that quinine, when properly used, is really an almost harmless *vegetable* product, which acts on malarial poisoning, not by great strength, but through its antidotal influence, just as water, an agent harmless enough to drink or bathe in, acts on fire.

One of the greatest hardships you will have to endure is the tendency of people who have suffered protracted sickness, to blame you or your medicine for any permanent impairment or stubborn symptoms remaining after illnesses, instead of recognizing the fact that they are the legitimate effects of disease.

Reproach is often unjustly heaped on physicians and on medicine by people living in malarious districts, who sicken with this or that malarial affection, send for a physician, and get well, and might remain so, but being still surrounded by malaria, they again inhale it and are again poisoned. This they erroneously call "a return," instead of a re-poisoning. Of course, while the laws of nature remain as they are, you can no more promise future immunity to convalescents with an agued frame who remain in malarious regions, than you can promise the anxious sailor that future winds will not again create waves, or the uneasy farmer that recurring frosts will not again nip his exposed plants.

Malaria is usually contracted at night, but many people are not aware of the fact that it can also be caught in the daytime, and should be put on their guard.

It is proper, and your duty, to advise a person to change his abode if his health require, or to relinquish an occupation if it be injurious to him. Also to discourage him from exciting employments, or from pursuing riches when his health is thereby jeopardized; but remember that these are extremely delicate subjects.

Keep yourself fully informed concerning dietetics and hygienics, the comparative healthfulness of different regions, the presence or absence of malaria at different seasons and places, etc.; also regarding the various health trips and summer resorts. Familiarize yourself with the constituents and peculiarities of the various mineral waters and of the uses of each; with the comparative advantages of seaside and mountain trips, and with the classes of invalids to be benefited by one or the other; also with the various baths—hot, cold, tepid, Russian, Turkish, electric, vapor, etc., and the comparative advantages of the various hospitals, asylums, sanitaria, retreats, etc.; for these matters belong strictly to the province of medicine, and it is particularly desirable to understand them, because they are subjects that concern the better and more desirable classes of patients, many of whom are semi-invalids, with whom you will often have to make hygiene, medicinal waters, trips, etc., go hand in hand with medication.

Be cautious in advising persons far gone with dangerous or hopeless maladies to leave their homes to undergo the discomforts of travel to distant points in search
of health, unless there are positive reasons for the
change, or decided probabilities that improvement or
restoration will follow. The risk of death away from
home, family and kindred, or of a return made worse by
the inevitable fatigues and exposures of travel, is not to
be assumed without full consideration.

Be chary of even sending people from their homes to
hospitals, unless you are perfectly sure the management
is humane and skilful. " Be it ever so humble, there is
no place like home." To carry a sick person to a hospital, deprive him of his friends, neighbors and compan-
ions, restrict his freedom and subject him to hum-drum
hospital rules ; expose him possibly to the public gaze,
clothe him hospital-fashion and put him on diet prepared at regulation hours by stranger hands that know
not his peculiarities or tastes, his likes and dislikes—
if he be a person of domestic tastes and sensitive
disposition, with a strong attachment to his home and
its surroundings, such a change would be most hurtful
and injudicious, and could scarcely fail to aggravate his
disease.

The belief that taking water or ice is dangerous in
fever is still very general. People are wonderfully slow
to recognize the fact that water, whether applied exter-
nally or swallowed in small quantities at a time, is one
of nature's greatest remedies in fever, especially if the
patient has a craving for it.

If a person sweats more during sleep than at any
other time, it is a sure sign of weakness.

You will often be asked, "Doctor, may he eat anything he wishes?" If you think that ordinary food will
do him no injury, be careful to answer, "Yes, he can have
any *simple* thing he wishes." Were you to say he can
have *anything*, it would include pickles, radishes, cheese,
ham, sausage, and a great many other indigestible things
that might injure or kill him; adding the adjective
simple will protect both him and you.

When you are busy and wish to make a short visit,
do not tell the patient so, or exhibit a hurried or abrupt
demeanor, but begin promptly to ask the necessary pues-
tions, and do not let the conversation become desultory
or in any way digress from his case till you have learned
all that is necessary. If the subject of the weather is
broached, answer as if you were considering it only in
reference to its influence on the patient, then go back to
his case. Economize time thus; but if your patient is
at all ill, neither mention your haste, nor show that you
are in a hurry until you have made your examination
and written your prescription. After that, if you depart
promptly he will not feel that your hurry has caused
any inattention to his case.

It will often vex you, when you are busy and time
is precious, to be kept waiting below stairs while the
people in the sick-room prim and prepare to receive you,
with as much prudery as if the surroundings, rather
than the patient, were the object of your visit. Show
every one the respect due to rank and sex, but manage
to let such people know that your time is too precious to
waste, and must be divided somewhat equally among
those whom you are attending.

Never assign as a reason for being habitually late in visiting a patient that you are over-busy. Every one wants a physician who is in active experience and engrossed in practice, but no one is willing to be habitually slighted or crowded out. It is an excellent rule always to let patients know at your visit when they may expect your next visit, and go as near that time as circumstances will allow. To do so gives satisfaction and prevents anxiety, and you will upon going generally find them prepared to see you without detention or flurry.

It is very important always to ask to see the patient's medicine as soon as possible at your visit. Ascertain by both inspection and inquiry whether it has been taken according to your directions, *before* you express any opinion of the patient's progress. If you neglect to do so you may be caught confidently ascribing benefits to prescriptions that have not been filled, or to remedies that have either been thrown out of the window or emptied into the garbage-box, and you will become the victim of a never-to-be-forgotten joke.

School yourself to avoid crude remedies, and to cultivate conservative rather than radical ones. Throw gross physic to the dogs. Fame for not being heroic and not giving much strong medicine, is just now a splendid item in a physician's reputation, one that might almost be adopted as a corner-stone. Of course, in cases where duty actually requires you to act promptly, or to use powerful remedies heroically, take the responsibility and do whatever is proper without shrinking.

Avoid polypharmacy. It is much better to order some single remedy, or a combination of which you know the physiological effect, than to give an indefinite medley on the ancient blunderbuss principle.

It is highly proper to warn people of dangers to the public health, and to devise means to prevent or remove such dangers; also to teach patients the importance of right living, proper dress, correct diet, pure air, and drainage, that they may preserve their health; but it is neither just nor wise to teach any but medical students, the secrets of our art. Especially avoid giving self-sufficient people therapeutical points that they can thereafter resort to and ignore the physician. If you do, they will soon become opinionated and imagine they know as much about medicine as you do, or more, and not only take your bread from you, but make hobbies of what you teach them, and trifle with them, till, in bad cases, the patient's disease is fatally seated. It is not your duty to cheat either yourself or other physicians out of legitimate practice by supplying this person and that one with a pharmacopœia for general use. If compelled to give people remedies under a simple form, study to do so in such a way as not to increase their self-conceit and make them feel that they know enough to practice self-medication and dispense with your services; use whatever strategy is necessary to prevent such persons from taking unfair advantage of your prescriptions.

It is unwise to instruct a person with rheumatism, gonorrhœa, ulcers, sore mouth, sprains, or any affliction whatever, to get five or ten cents' worth of this or that remedy, to mix for himself, unless it be one of the very worthy poor; because people are sure to abuse such orders, and to try to teach every one similarly afflicted how to treat himself. It is better either to let such persons have the medicine from your office, or to write them a prescription for it, with instructions neither to repeat nor lend.

In prescribing, and even in speaking of medicines, you should use officinal names, and not popular titles, unless there is some special reason for using a synonym.

Do not patronize any of the semi-legitimate pharmaceutical catchpennies that are now flooding our nostrum-ridden land. For instance, if a patient needs beef, let him eat beef, or have beef soup or beef extract made for him; if he needs wine, order for him a suitable quantity of the kind which you prefer; if he needs iron, prescribe the kind and the dose that you think proper, and do not make yourself a mere distributer of some enterprising fellow's ready-made "beef, wine and iron," which cheats the pharmacist out of all chance of exercising his profession, and relieves him of all responsibility in the matter, since he has nothing to do but hand it out, in a mechanical fashion, to customers, just as the grocer hands out soap, matches and tobacco.

The same hat cannot fit every head, or the same shoe answer for every foot, neither can the proportion of ingredients in a ready-made combination suit every patient. Indeed, what would cure one might kill another.

Resolve never to prescribe a proprietary remedy, or one covered by a trade-mark; it is better to avoid the use of all such ready-prepared remedies, whether trade-mark, proprietary or quack, whether advertised to the profession or to the public, whether the so-called formula and the dose are given or not. If you order A's emulsion, B's lozenges, C's cod-liver oil, D's pills and E's bitters, to patients, they will, by association, soon think that X's sarsaparilla, Y's buchu, and Z's liver regulator, also meet with professional approval. Determine that you will not aid any speculator in life and health, to "strike a trade" in your families; and chiefly for the reason that *their nostrums do more harm than good;* also for the lesser reason, that justice to yourself and every other physician requires you to avoid prescribing or telling patients of preparations that enable them afterwards to snap their fingers in your face and renew them as often as they please.

Endeavor to have your prescription labelled so as to prevent indiscriminate renewal, as well as to prevent mistakes in their administration; when they are very important, have the name of the patient put on the label.

Remember this : The very best time to tell a patient not to renew a prescription is while writing it. If you fear it will be renewed against your wish, stop short while writing and remark to him that it will be a good remedy, or make some other true remark about it, but that he must take only one bottle, or that it must not be renewed. Your order given at that time will seem to be founded on some motive other than that of protecting your own pecuniary interest, will impress him strongly, and will be invariably obeyed; this is probably the most effective of all plans to prevent prescriptions from being renewed and adopted as a regular resort in similar cases. With this exception, make it a rule not to talk, listen to, nor answer questions while writing prescriptions.

Never write a prescription carelessly. Cultivate the habit of scrutinizing everything you write after it is written, to assure yourself that there is neither omission nor mistake, and sign your name or initials to every prescription, but not till you have satisfied yourself that it is as intended.

In consultation, the prescription agreed upon should be written by the regular attendant, and if the consultant is still present, should be submitted to him for inspection; but only the regular attendant's name or initials should be signed to it.

A very, very useful rule in many cases is to name the hours at which medicine is to be taken; thus, if it is to be taken every five hours, instead of writing "a teaspoonful every five hours," write "take a teaspoonful at 7, 12, 5, and 10 o'clock daily."

Remember, when giving directions in regard to doses, that spoons and drops vary greatly in size. A patient can save much trouble and uncertainty in cases where medicine is to be taken for any length of time, by getting a graduated tumbler or medicine glass, which is both convenient and precise. A minim is a definite quantity, a drop is not; therefore, in prescribing potent fluids, you should order minims instead of drops.

Neither alarm your patients nor their friends, nor risk the dangers of the chloral, opium, or other bad habit by allowing them to know they are taking such articles.

If you instruct a patient how to use the hypodermic

syringe on himself, or to inhale chloroform or ether, or give him chloral, opium or alcoholic liquors loosely, if he has any predisposition at all towards them, he will probably adopt the habit; if he does, you will surely and *deservedly* incur the blame. The slaves of such habits always cast the blame for their acquired passion, or their enslavement, on the physicians who first ordered or used the drug with them, if they have any ground at all for doing so.

Hypodermic medication not only has its place and power, which make it at times indispensable, but also has various drawbacks, that should prevent its indiscriminate use; among other evils connected with it is this, that those who are charmed by it, or have become habituated to it, are apt to harass and worry you for its use at all hours, day and night. It is a real hardship after doing your day's work that you must go and administer a hypodermic of morphia to A. at 9 o'clock P. M., to B. at 10, and to C. at 11 o'clock, and probably be called from bed again to administer to one or all of them before morning.

Much of this is not only a hardship but a nuisance. Far better is it for both the patient and yourself that you order anodynes by the mouth or rectum for such patients, than risk what may prove to be a fatal charm.

CHAPTER VIII.

Self-reliance and self-possession are very important elements of success. Nothing under the sun will cause people to rely on you more readily and permanently than to see you rely on yourself. Be not arrogant, or self-conceited, but always hide your doubts, hesitations, uncertainties, and apprehensions as completely as possible.

Never turn your cases over to *"specialists,"* unless they have features which render it an actual duty to do so. If you timidly refer every case of eye disease to the oculists, every uterine case to the gynæcologists, ear cases to the aurists, surgical to surgeons, nervous affections to neurologists, throat complaints to laryngologists, mental afflictions to alienists, and so on throughout the list, you will lessen your own field of activity, and instead of gaining as much experience with one affection as another, you will soon lose all familiarity with the diseases that specialists treat, and will degenerate into a mere distributer of cases, a medical adviser instead of a medical attendant—studying everybody's interest except your own, and making reputations for them out of that which sinks your own individuality, depletes your own purse, and destroys your own fame. A good rule is this:

[174]

whenever a case proves wholly unmanageable by usual treatment, or is so grave in prognosis as undoubtedly to require broader shoulders than yours to bear the responsibility, either call in a specialist to aid in its management, or turn it over entirely to him. Timidity and rashness are both bad traits in a physician, but the former is the greater drawback.

When you transfer any one from your care to a specialist's, always do so either by a consultation, a letter, or a personal interview with him, that he may learn directly from you your diagnosis, prognosis, treatment, etc. You will thereby give him the advantage of what you know of the case, and also prevent the risk of an injury to your reputation from an apparently radical difference of opinion between him and yourself; besides, it secures your graceful retirement from the case.

Be careful to make your patients fully understand that in turning their cases over to a surgeon or specialist you do not cease to be their physician for future sickness, and that you have only turned them over *for that special affection.*

Ask for a consultation in all important cases in which knotty problems are presented, or where there exists any doubt as to the diagnosis, and in all cases where you think either the patient's interest, his lack of improvement, or a division of the responsibility demands it. When from any cause you see a necessity for one arising, try, if possible, to anticipate the family by being the first to propose it.

Consultations lessen personal responsibility. When you have bad surgical and other cases among your personal friends or relatives, or so near home as to involve you personally or socially, or in a neighborhood in which a group of patients are likely to be unfavorably impressed if the result is not good, it is especially necessary and wise to call a consulting physician, even though you have him to come but once—if for no other reason, to satisfy the persons concerned.

If possible, always have physicians selected as consultants who will second your efforts by their knowledge and skill, and who will at the same time be likely to harmonize with you in the management of your cases; for their sympathy and kindly support may be highly necessary to the patient's welfare and to your own reputation.

Be punctual to the minute in keeping consultation engagements. You have no right to waste another's time in such cases; or to impose upon him the necessity of awaiting idly for you at the place of meeting.

In your consultations you will often feel great anxiety and suspense while waiting to see whether the consulting physician will be fair towards you, or whether he will shrewdly expose your deficiencies to a few, to be told to many, till you are killed in the estimation of all to whom the case is related. To the honor of our profession be it said, that the vast majority of its older members are not only punctilious, but really kind to the deserving on these occasions.

A radical change of diagnosis and of treatment, as the result of a first consultation, often naturally impresses upon the laity the idea that the previous diagnosis or treatment has been either faulty or actually wrong, and no material change should be proposed or allowed *at that time*, unless some real necessity requires it. As a rule, the fewer the apparent changes resulting from a first consultation, the better for the regular attendant's reputation; especially if he be a *young* physician.

When a consulting physician is designated and called at your request, you should see that the payment of his fee is not neglected; you might with propriety broach the subject to those who are to pay the bill, before he quits. This can be done by privately informing them that his charges will probably be somewhat less if paid at his last visit than if they wait for him to send a bill, which might then be for the maximum amount.

You can, in such a case, speak much more plainly for your brother physician called at your instance than you could for yourself. His relations to the case suppose him to have nothing in view but the welfare of the patient, and to be thinking only of the scientific and therapeutical aspects of the case, and not at all of his fees. Prompt settlement of the consultant's fee will sometimes even bring about a more prompt payment of your own.

Unless the consulting physician gets his fees cash, or you are aware that special arrangements exist for their payment, be very careful to inform the people as soon as he ceases coming, or at any rate before the time arrives for sending them *your* bill, whether he will send his bill separately from yours or not. If you neglect to explain this to them, they will almost surely think you ought to pay him out of your fee, and a misunderstanding will result as to whether you or they must pay his bill.

12

Whenever, to please the patient or his friends, you give up other engagements in order to meet another physician in consultation, it is proper for you to charge for such service twice as much as for an ordinary visit, or perhaps even as much as the consultant does for his services ; for you have all the details to carry out and all the communications to make, and in consequence are entitled to extra compensation.

In dispensing with the consulting physician when his services are no longer necessary, take care to make him feel that it is done amicably.

Remember that you have no right to object to a patient's having other advice besides your own whenever he insists upon it; but also that you have an undoubted right to refuse to consult with any one whom you deem unprofessional, or unsuited for the case, any one who is personally objectionable to you, or in whose keeping you deem your reputation and interests unsafe. If you are attending a case and such an one is pressed upon you, you have a perfect right to retire. Fortunately, such dilemmas are very rare.

Do not refuse to consult with foreign physicians, doctresses, colored physicians, or any others, provided they are regular practitioners, or even with undergraduates, if they are advancing regularly towards their degree. You, as a physician, hold a quasi-official position in the community, and, in the discharge of your duties, should know nothing of national enmities, race prejudices, political strife, or sectarian differences ; you have no moral right to turn your back on sick and suffering humanity, by refusing to add your knowledge and skill to that of *any* honorable, liberal-minded person who practises medicine, if his professional acquirements and ethical tenets give him a claim to work in the professional field. It is not only unmanly to make a class distinction and throw obstacles in the path of the less favored, but such a spirit is wholly incompatible with the objects of our profession (which is a liberal one), and at direct variance with the spirit of science, which is cosmopolitan, and in its efforts to diminish suffering and baffle death knows neither caste, pride, nor prejudice, and has no limits except those of truth and duty.

But while you give the right hand of fellowship to every *regular* honorable physician, no matter what his misfortunes or how great his deficiencies, you must, on the other hand, remember that medicine is a liberal profession, and refuse it to any one whose pride, prejudice, or limited creed, or avowed or notorious hostility to our profession, prevents him from accepting every known fact and employing all known remedies. Refuse fellowship with any one and every one who cannot honestly say his mind is wide open for the reception of all truth, and that his hand shall not refuse to use anything and everything that may be needed for the benefit of the suffering. When called to a case in which the attendant cannot do this, let his retirement be one of the conditions on which you will assume charge.

You may be called to a case of emergency, viz. an alarming hemorrhage, poisoning, or difficult labor, and on reaching it find an irregular practitioner or quack in attendance; in such cases, the path of duty is plain, for, owing to the great and urgent danger to life, the higher law of humanity will require you temporarily to set aside éthics and etiquette, and to unite your efforts with your chance associate's. Treat him, then, with courtesy, but studiously avoid private consultations or whispering conversation with him, or any other act that might imply association in consultation.

Thus you see there is not only no antagonism between medical ethics and humanity, but that they allow and cover any act honestly performed for the benefit of humanity.

Fortunately, the indications for rational treatment are generally so very clear in such cases that no one can ignore them. If the Irregular has assumed charge before your arrival and is pursuing proper treatment, or agrees to the proper treatment suggested by you, that is all you can ask ; for instance, if the patient has received a terrible burn and linseed oil and lime water are being applied, or other rational treatment, endorse it and encourage a continuation in the same line, but if your accidental colleague is a hydropath and favors a wet pack because he is morbid on the use of water, or a homœopath and advocates a lotion of cantharides because they burn and blister well people, it is your duty to your patient and also to yourself unyieldingly to insist that a rational course shall be pursued, if you are to take part in the case. Be cautious but firm in dealing with such contingencies, and it is due both to your self-respect and that which you owe the profession, that you terminate the unnatural connection—of course in a gentlemanly way—as soon as the great urgency will admit.

Some of the unreasoning laity may think you are illiberal in refusing to fraternize and consult with Irregular practitioners, notwithstanding these have voluntarily separated themselves from the profession and assumed a name intended to tell the public that their system differs from ours, and that they are hostile to us. Remember that our refusal is not from a false sense of dignity, or from prejudice, but that the great principle which underlies it is this : as lovers of *all truth*, we have no fixed, no unchangeable creed, but hail with delight every etiological and therapeutical discovery, no matter by whom made, and take by the hand *any one* who is liberal enough to consecrate his life's labor to the relief of the sick ; but when we know that a certain person, even if he has a diploma, circumscribes himself and practises a botanical system *only*, or homœopathic system *only*, or a hydropathic system *only*, or any other *one-idea* system *only*, and is so tied down and limited to that, by his love, bigotry or prejudice, that he *denies* the usefulness of all other known and honorable means of aiding the sick, and endeavors to poison the public mind against all other systems but his own—all rational physicians esteem such an one as *too illiberal* to be a true physician, and justly exclude him as unsuitable for fellowship with those who profess to love all truth, and whilst he remains confined within the narrow limits of his own seclusion, endeavor to themselves steadily pursue the path of true science and progress.

If, on the other hand, he uses the remedies that rational medicine affords, yet adopts the cloak of an " ism," simply as an advertising dodge to make the public believe that he practises in some manner the direct opposite of ourselves, and thereby assists our enemies to lessen public esteem for regular medicine, and to create hatred towards us as its followers, he is guilty of fraud, and you should, even on the ground of morality, refuse to countenance him.

When people ask you "what school you practise," you may very properly answer that you are simply a PHYSICIAN, that you belong to no sect and are limited to no cut-and-dried creed, that you try to be *rational* and, like the bee, take the honey of truth wherever you find it; that as rational, liberal physicians, the regular profession, to which you belong, maintain perfect freedom of opinion and practice, and unlike the various "limited schools," have no articles of faith, which they impose on any one, but accept all truths, whether winnowed from past experience, or discovered, either scientifically or empirically, in our own day; that you, as one of its representatives, stand ready to receive and utilize any and every valuable discovery, no matter when or by whom made.

This flexibility explains why REGULAR MEDICINE IS ONE OF THE THREE LIBERAL PROFESSIONS, and why the humane and benevolent physician takes rank with the learned expounder of the law and with the worthy man who inculcates religion.

To this trio of professions was long ago applied the term "LIBERAL," because all three require the utmost perfection of character in their members, and because devotees of law, religion and medicine have, in all ages, pursued them as freemen, with hands unfettered and tongue untied, subject to no bonds, except those of TRUTH. If at any time during your career, any sect or school arises, no matter how great or how humble its pretensions, if it has even one grain of wheat to a bushel of chaff, it is your duty to seize the grain of wheat and utilize it, and cast the chaff to the winds. This adaptability is our strength and our glory, and is the element that will make regular, liberal, rational medicine exist as long as there are sickness and suffering in the world, and is the feature that distinguishes genuine medicine from "new schools," isms and pathies.

Remember that the door of the profession is not only open to the newly graduated, but to every one who has the necessary educational and moral qualifications, even though he has been allied, whether from ignorance or choice, with schools which profess antagonism to the profession; in the latter case he is at perfect liberty at any time to enter our ranks by dropping his distinguishing creed, abandoning the hostility to the profession which it implies, and allowing ethical rules to govern his conduct: no conversion, no surrender of private opinion is at all necessary.

Be exact in everything that relates to consultations. Let them always be formal and strictly private; consult within a room that is, if possible, isolated from intrusion; exchange thoughts in an undertone and out of the sight and the hearing of eavesdroppers. Never allow any one to be present, except the physicians engaged in it.

Remember that consultations are called for the purpose of deciding for the *future*, not to criticize the past; but if you are called to consult in a case and find the attending physican is suffering unmerited odium for his previous management, every principle of honor should impel you to *volunteer* to defend him.

Let all that follows a consultation show that you act in concert and that it is the result of joint action, and never express an individual opinion of a case seen in consultation, except in strict accordance with the Code. If you do, those whom you address may, either unintentionally or purposely, misinterpret what you say, or otherwise involve you.

Remember that if you agree sufficiently to continue in joint attendance, you are in duty bound to uphold each other, and to refrain from hints and insinuations likely to affect confidence in your fellow attendant.

If you are requested by letter, or by a messenger, to prescribe for an out-of-town patient who is not under the care of any other physician, it is perfectly professional to do so, if you wish, even though you may never have seen the case.

If a professional friend for any reason requests you to see a case with him, not so much for the patient's sake as for his own benefit, you should lend him a ready and willing hand, and that, too, without expectation of a fee.

Avoid reviling the individual members of the profession, or the profession itself, or telling people of the mistakes and discreditable dilemmas of yourself or others; and also avoid decrying and ridiculing medicine to the laity, and boasting of your own and the general ignorance of disease and remedies; and suppress all other fulsome confessions. When a physician speaks thus, he means it *relatively* only; means to say, that he is aware and willing to confess that medicine has its natural limits and is not an exact science, and that the application of therapeutics is but an art. The public cannot appreciate the sense in which such confessions are made, and they are taken up by our enemies as quickly as an empty sponge takes up water, and work ounces of harm to physicians who make them and pounds of harm to the profession at large; because all who hear or read them conclude that medical practice is only a network of uncertainty, inconsistencies and confusion, and ever after either do not employ physicians at all, or do so with utter disrespect and distrust.

You know there is no such thing practically as a perfectly straight line, plane surface, regular curve, exact sphere, or uniform solid; yet you never hear the engineer or surveyor boasting of it in reckless language as if to belittle his own profession.

The truth is, physicians are far more imperfect than physic. For instance: there are undoubtedly medicines whose action is *diuretic;* but *diuretics* may be given when not indicated, or the *diuretic* given may not be the proper one, or it may be wrong in quantity, or be given at improper intervals, or proper restrictions for its use may not be enforced. Now none of these errors are justly chargeable to the class of medicines we call *diuretics,* nor to the art of medicine, but are plainly due either to the physician's bad judgment, or to his ignorance. The fact is, all studious physicians know of very nearly the same remedies, but skill in curing with them consists in selecting the proper ones, in proportioning the dose, judging correctly the time for use, etc. Just so, different persons essaying to paint will exhibit dif-

ferent degrees of success; one possessed of natural apti-
tude or special smartness will attain wonderful skill,
another less apt will reach mediocrity, while a third
will fail entirely in his attempts and quit in disgust—
this difference in result being due not to a difference
in the material or colors at the command of each, but
to the more or less perfect judgment and skill shown
by each in selecting and using them.

Ability to determine accurately the condition of a
patient, and to conceive and do the right thing for him
at the right time, is the essence of skill, constitutes the
chief difference between successful and unsuccessful physicians, and explains the reason why the prescriptions
of some physicians are much more valuable than those
of others.

A proper use of medicines, and not a wholesale re-
nunciation of them, is a leading characteristic of a good
physician. When you hear of a physician who wishes
to be considered especially clear, or ahead of others, or
extraordinarily fair in his opinions, boasting that he is
skeptical, "does not believe in drugs," "depends on
nature," etc., you can safely conclude that in his zeal to
become a medical philosopher, or to coquette with somebody else's opinion, he has lapsed in his materia medica,
or overstates his credulity, or that his usefulness has run
to seed.

Does the mariner lose his faith in navigation because
ships are tossed by the winds and waves and sometimes
wrecked by uncontrollable storms? or does the farmer
deny the fertility of the soil because his neighbor has
neglected the proper season for planting and correct

ways of cultivating; or does he lose his faith in agriculture because droughts and grasshoppers sometimes ruin his crops? Would any worthy sailor fold his arms and do nothing while the storm raged, or any philosophical farmer neglect to plant again when the season returned, because the sailor's brightest hopes are sometimes crushed and the farmer's fairest prospects are often blighted?

Is there a physician on earth who would let intermittent and remittent fevers take their course without drugs, or who would let the syphilitic and other poisons develop, or progress unchecked? Is there a graduate anywhere who confesses he can do *nothing* for pain or for fever, for nervous complaints, for digestive affections or chest diseases; nothing for circulatory disorders, delirium, insomnia, headache, epilepsy, hysteria, gout, neuralgia, worms, colic, acidity, peritonitis, constipation, diarrhœa, anœmia, scurvy, etc.?

The end and aim of medical practice is to relieve, to cure, and to prevent death, therefore if there is a physician in the land who has never seen medicines restore health or prolong life, who does not sincerely believe in his power to benefit by drugs some of the twenty-four hundred diseases and modes of decay to which mankind is subject, he should at once and forever, for conscience' sake, and for the sake of the afflicted, take down his sign and no longer pretend to practise.

The tolerance of disease has greatly increased in the last few decades, and is still increasing, and medical theories and practice are undergoing great changes. The advance of scientific observation is constantly teaching us to distinguish more clearly between the multitude of simple self-limited cases daily met with and the few that threaten a fatal issue, and *of course* we of to-day use much lighter remedies for the former class than our predecessors did ; but it is doubtful whether in real sicknesses we have *lessened* the doses half as much as some imagine. You now give twelve or fifteen grains of quinia daily for an intermittent fever, where physicians formerly gave half an ounce or an ounce of crude bark containing but six or twelve grains. You give to-day the same dose of opium, or its representative, morphia, when that drug is indicated, as they gave a hundred years ago, the same quantity of castor oil at a dose, and about the same throughout the entire materia medica. The great difference is, that we do not now prescribe vaguely or rashly, and when cases are obscure or undeveloped, our treatment is tentative instead of heroic.

We of to-day know better than our predecessors the natural history of disease, and are aware of the almost infinite resources of nature, and that three in every ten of those who send for physicians need no positive medication, and that nine of the ten would get well sooner or later by proper hygiene and intelligent nursing and dieting if there were not a drug in the world, and consequently we are naturally prescribing less and less. In acute diseases, and especially those of children, we now, in many cases, trust chiefly to nature, and see them get well from what look to be hopeless conditions, almost as if by magic, and these cases constitute a majority of those that seem to be restored to rosy health by therapeutical illusions and quack medicines, which contain nothing of an active perturbating character.

The deduction to be drawn from these facts is that the physician may show as much—nay, more—skill in withholding drugs when not needed as in giving them when they are.

CHAPTER IX.

" Together let us beat this ample field,
  Try what the open, what the covert yield."—POPE.

Aim earnestly to please every one's taste and ideas of medicine as far as is compatible with safety. Bear ever in mind that a man is something more than a stomach and body, and constantly study the use of psychological aids, and try to compel your patient to assist in curing his own case. Also avoid over-drugging, and remember that those who have been most fond of medicine, often become suddenly surfeited and undergo a complete revulsion against both medicine and physicians. How can this be wondered at when even too long a continuation of beefsteak, partridge, oysters, or other choice food, causes disgust and utter loathing even in well people?

This tendency in the human mind has in recent times received an unfortunate illustration at our expense, and in this way: Satiated and disgusted with Humoral Pathology and its crude and over-active measures, administered too often without regard to caprice or palate, the majority of people were anxiously wishing for almost any change, when lo! THE HOMŒOPATH appeared, and offered as a substitute a new do-nothing system, resting on a creed composed of one logical and two pseudo-logical tenets, which admirably serves to advertise both system and disciple, and to amuse and employ those who trust to the latter, without offending either eye, palate or stomach; depending really on unassisted nature to do the work; if adhered to, allowing cases that it cannot restore unaided, to become complicated or chronic, or to succumb and be added to the list of those who die of preventable deaths.

So strong is the popular reaction against extreme and unnecessary medication, that this silly system has flourished to a most astonishing degree, and may be regarded as the greatest medical delusion of the nineteenth century. There can be no doubt, however, that its career would long since have terminated had the profession not been so loath to accommodate itself to the demands of fashion, particularly with reference to medication in slight and imaginary cases. But rational physicians are at last arousing to the importance of this subject, and are conforming to the changed popular sentiment. They are at the same time administering more concentrated and palatable forms of medicines in serious cases, and thanks to the labors of the many devoted workers in the field of medical science, and the light which has been thus shed upon the subject, are enabled to effect cures with greater certainty, promptness and safety than ever before. The result is that many of the erring are being brought back from the ranks of the " isms " and " pathies," to faith in a legitimate and rational system of practice. Determine that you will bear your share in the good work, by devoting time and study to the means of rendering therapeutics pleasant and acceptable to patients.

You are of course bound by the most sacred obligations to use your best judgment and endeavors for the good of every one who comes under your professional care, but neither the Code of Ethics nor the Code of Honor forbids your sailing before popular breezes, provided you violate no principle of truth and justice.

No honest man could compromise a matter of principle, *i. e.*, knowingly quit the right for the wrong; yet it is sometimes very foolish not to compromise a matter of policy. In medicine the second best course often becomes the best because the patient prefers it, and although you can neither believe nor follow Hahnemann's nonsense and follies, you *can* follow *the fashion of the day*, and *can* give to every fastidious or squeamish patient the smallest and most pleasant dose that his safety will permit, and *can* avoid giving any one crude remedies to a disgusting degree.

Now, although homœopathy is somewhat fashionable, when a case actually requires medication you can make very little if any rational use of its so-called principles, which rest on the following foolish creed:—1*st. Curative remedies for the sick can be selected only by a study of provings on persons in health. 2d. Every remedy must be given by itself. 3d. The similar and single remedy must be given in its minimum dose, i. e., the smallest dose sufficient to effect a cure in the case.* These are the three legs upon which Hahnemannism is supposed to stand; an *essential* triune, an *inseparable* unit. Violation of any one of these principles by the faithful is a confessed rejection of the whole.

You will observe at a glance that this creed is exactly two-thirds nonsense; that the first and second postulates are sophistical and untrue, and hence should be rejected, and that the last, *i. e.*, to give the smallest dose that will answer the purpose, is a rule which nobody denies. Every rational person, whether physician or not, has recognized ever since the days of Methuselah, that it is useless to pour seven buckets of water on a fire when he is sure that three will put it out; which piece of common sense is equally true in medicine, and cannot in any manner be monopolized by the homœopath.

Contrary to what many unthinking people believe, this creed gives the homœopaths perfect liberty to give either an atom or an ounce of lime, salt, sugar, or anything else, at a dose, provided they proceed on the homœopathic principle of similars; and the *question* whether they, or you, or any one else does, or does not practise homœopathy *does not* depend upon the size of the dose at all. They might give an ounce of a medicine in cases in which you would give but a grain. Their ounce would not make them *rational* physicians, nor your grain make you a homœopathist.

Here is the true test as to whether you are practising homœopathically or not: Were you to examine a patient and ask yourself, *What is the best treatment known to the world for a case like the one before me?* and give him that, without regard to either creed or boundary, you would be practising *rational* medicine. If, on the contrary, you were to examine a case and ask yourself: *What article would produce a totality of symptoms similar to these in a well person?* and give him the one which you thought would come nearest to doing this, you would be practising homœopathically. Now, it is safe

13

to conclude that if you practise medicine forty years, you will never sit down by an ill man's bedside and ask yourself seriously, "What agent would produce a disease similar to this, or symptoms similar to these, in a well person?" and attempt to simulate it in your treatment. Therefore take care to remember that, no matter how small your dose, even though, in the exercise of your privilege, you prescribe only teaspoonful doses of *aqua pura*, or let your patient smell an empty bottle, it will not be practising *homœopathically*.

It is also safe to predict that while reason remains your mistress, you will never seriously entertain, much less follow, a system of medicine that in dogmatically seeking *similars*, arrives at poison oak as a remedy for erysipelas, croton oil as a remedy for cholera infantum, mercury for mumps, tartar emetic for typhoid-pneumonia, opium for apoplexy, strychnia for convulsions, and a countless myriad more of similar nonsense.

Study the "Organon of Medicine" and "The Lesser Writings," by Samuel Hahnemann—"Homœopathy Fairly Represented," by William Henderson, M. D.— Hull's "Jahr"—Hughes' "Pharmaco-Dynamics"— Johnson's "Therapeutic Key," the works of Hering, Lippe, Guernsey, and other leading homœopathic authorities, and you will learn that a genuine homœopath prescribes according to what he believes to be a grand natural law which Hahnemann by his genius discovered, and which is comprehended in the phrase "*similia similibus curantur*," or, like cures like.

Now while it is universally admitted that quinia cures intermittent fever, who ever heard of its being homœopathic to the periodic feature of that disease? and yet where is the homœopath that does not, in periodic fevers, administer sugar-coated quinine pills in full doses? Podophyllin is the favorite cathartic of the homœopath. Does it cause constipation? No intelligent physician would contend that it did. That morphia relieves that great enemy to human life and health, pain—is one of the best attested facts of medical observation; will any homœopath dare say that it causes pain? The same may be said of mercury in syphilis, and of cod-liver oil in scrofula and phthisis. These are not stray assertions, they are monumental facts. What then becomes of the law of similars?

Compare Hahnemann and the so-called natural law, published by him in the Organon in 1810—all the way through, with Copernicus, Newton, and other real discoverers of nature's laws, and you will find his grandiloquent pretensions resting on so slight a foundation that it will strongly remind you of an inverted pyramid, and you will then fully realize what an amazing folly Hahnemann's so-called natural law is, and *why* we reject it, and will also see how men can mistake the workings of nature, and of faith and credulity, for the effects of—infinitesimal globules—till their delusions carry them to visionary regions and completely pervert their reasoning powers.

You will discover that nine out of ten of those who run after sugar powders and pellets know absolutely nothing at all about the Hahnemannian principles and calculations, and take them themselves and give them to their families solely because they are fashionable, novel, cheap, easily taken, and prevent running to the druggist with expensive prescriptions.

Another of Hahnemann's grand and imposing laws, the dynamization of medicines, the one that he and his followers formerly praised most in proselyting, and which was used by them as a wonder-creating something made of nothing, is a farcical parody on an old well-known principle in medicine.

These notions of his not only contradict reason and violate common sense, but conflict with fixed mathematical laws, since a part cannot be greater than the whole. The truth is, the so-called dynamization of medicines bears about as much relation to the science of medicine, as the kaleidoscope does to the science of astronomy.

The novelty of globulism and attenuations, like spiritualism and mesmerism, aims at two of the strongest qualities of the human **mind**, qualities that we might honestly utilize more fully—*the love of the mysterious and novel.*

As previously stated, **nothing** under heaven prevents you from giving whatever you think best for your patient; whether its therapeutic action is similar, or antagonistic; but, if in so doing, you adopt a narrow or foolish dogma, or an exclusive system, and prejudice your mind against all other ascertained truths, your partisanship will fetter you, abridge your usefulness, and make you unfit for fellowship in liberal medicine. Thus, when Vincent Priessnitz, in trying to build a house of a single brick, shut his eyes to everything but hydropathy, and Samuel Hahnemann dogmatically tied himself to the homœopathic delusion, and rabidly denounced everything else, and Samuel Thompson in his exclusivism threw away everything but herbs, they lessened their own usefulness and that of all who follow them.

> "For never yet hath one attained
> To such perfection, but that time, and place,
> And use, have brought addition to his knowledge;
> Or made correction, or admonished him
> That he was ignorant of much which he
> Had thought he knew, or led him to reject
> What he had once esteemed of highest price."

Not a single department of medicine has yet reached scientific exactness, and possibly never will. *We*, as rational legitimate physicians, are striving hard to bring its various branches as *near* to perfection as possible, and are willing to learn medical truth and scientific wisdom wherever they can be found. When "New Schools," schisms or creeds arise, if they possess any new or valuable truths, or remedies of ascertained merit, no matter how great or how small, whether taken from the animal, vegetable or mineral kingdom, we instantly single them out and incorporate them with the great mass to swell the records of rational medicine, so that the medicine of to-day may be said to be a living, moving, growing thing, founded on all its yesterdays.

The homœopaths and all other Irregulars cunningly sneer at the regular profession and style us "The Old School," "Allopaths," etc., to make it appear to the public that every physician must belong to some special school, and that ours is merely one of these restricted creeds, old-fashioned and worn-out, with by-gone habits and ancient ways of thinking, which, though good enough in their day, are now altogether inadequate and behind the times. Their aim in doing this is, of course, to obtain the advantage of appearing to stand fully equal with us, just as, for instance, in religion one sect stands with reference to another, and in politics Republicans stand with Democrats. You know that nothing could be more false.

Remember that the title "Allopath" was the insignificant misnomer given to us by the great, the all-wise and infallible Hahnemann, as part of his little crusade for the destruction of all but his own dreamy system, and is applied to us opprobriously by his followers, with sinister motives; that it is both untrue and offensive, and is *not* recognized by regular physicians. Take care *promptly* to resent it when any one applies it to you through enmity, and to disown it and also tell of its falsity and hostile origin when applied through ignorance.

An allopathic physician would be one whose foolishly restricted creed required him to substitute some other disease for the one he was called upon to treat. There is probably not an allopathist in the world, and it is doubtful whether there ever was one.

Strange to say, now-a-days a section of the public, blinded by sophistry and swayed by false sentiment, instead of siding with them when they are right and turning against them when they are wrong, invariably sides with the "new school" or the quack, or anybody else, whenever a contest arises between them and us. Even a portion of the press, religious as well as secular, seem to delight in aiming sharp shafts at the regular profes-

sion, and creating popular sentiment in favor of its
enemies, by making invidious comparisons between its
modes of practice and theirs—telling of their wonderful
success, and of their steady growth in public confidence,
in highly colored terms. Editorial and other authorita-
tive productions are frequently written on our arbitrary
exclusiveness, our intolerant bigotry, etc.; our disagreements, too, are magnified and reported in a sensa-
tional way, all *apparently* to antagonize and decry us,
and enhance the interests of Irregulars and advertising
quacks.

You will find that if a person happens to get better,
even of an ordinary case, while under the care of an
Irregular, or when taking a quack medicine, it will receive
a thousand praises through the neighborhood; whereas
if twenty get well by your remedies, it will scarcely
excite a comment.

'Tis said the Chinese are so expert in making much
out of little, that they live and fatten on what a Cau-
casian wastes. In the same degree, Irregulars and
quacks thrive on the quickening influence of the emo-
tions, expectation, faith, hope, etc., which we, with our
minds fixed on more tangible aids, neglect far more than
we should. For proof of the mighty power of the mind
over the body, look at the liver pads, tractors, amulets,
charms, and dozens of other humbug agents in vogue,
which the young and old, black and white, educated and
illiterate, all kinds, classes and conditions of people, are
praising, almost as if they had fallen from the skies.

Fashion and wealth exert a powerful influence in
medical affairs, and unfortunately a certain portion of

the fashionable, wealthy and influential, favor and patronize almost every novelty, schism, or delusion in medicine, and make them popular and fashionable with the
unthinking herd, who are always ready to imitate their
superiors.

Many Irregulars have another source of éclat. They
magnify what we would call a slight cold, or a quinsy,
into a "congestion of the lungs," a "bronchial catarrh,"
a "touch of pneumonia," "diphtheria," or "post-nasal
catarrh." They dignify what we would call a disordered stomach into a "gastric affection," a wind colic
into "borborygmus," etc., for the cure of which huge
ailments they are fully credited and fully paid. There
is a fellow in our section who manages his patrons so
adroitly that he often actually reaps manifold more
credit and patronage for stopping a chill and fever in
seven days, than a true physician would for doing the
same in a day or two, and other ailments in proportion.
This effort to exaggerate their cures was apparent in the
famous Homœopathic Hospital Reports at Vienna, and
when discovered, vitiated their reliability altogether.

Another reason why Irregulars get cases is, that if a
physician grows tired of a case and loses interest, or the
patient gets tired of him and loses faith, the family is apt
to desire a change of physicians, and fearing the attendant would become offended were they to dismiss him and
employ one of his brethren, they get an Irregular, under
the belief that the physician will feel *less hurt* if they
dismiss him under the plea of trying "a different
system" of doctoring, than on any other pretext.

Another reason why Irregulars have partisans is that

there is always a sprinkling of extremists in every community, who for some cause or other are imbued with an unreasoning antagonism to the regular profession, who unite to abet and support any class or system which practises in opposition to it, and of course such demand creates a supply.

Again, a physician is sometimes compelled candidly to give a gloomy or despairing prognosis, and this is apt to cause a transfer of the case to some noisy quack who makes great professions and rosy promises.

Still another reason why they get patrons is this. They take care to announce that they cure by mild means or harmless methods, and not by complicated, painful or dangerous measures, bloody operations under anæsthetics or other *derniers ressorts* that science teaches *us* to use—against all of which they have, by fallacious statistics, aroused much of the existing foolish prejudice and abhorrence.

So great indeed is the popular dread of what doctors *might do*, that in choosing an attendant from among regular physicians, the nervous and the timid, who constitute *nine-tenths* of all the sick, are greatly inclined to shun all who treat heroically, and seek those who use moderate, even though less efficient means.

Homœopathy not only panders to whims, but also makes a specialty of poisoning the minds of its votaries, as well against the lancet, polypharmacy, and other needlessly active measures, as against *all* rational remedies, inclining them to attach undue importance to trivial affections, and to over-estimate the value of treatment therein, and creating a pathophobic watchfulness over the minutiæ of tneir health, and eventually making them morbidly anxious about every function, and filling their minds with a medley of imaginary and exaggerated afflictions which haunt them, like Banquo's ghost, wherever they go. You will often see perfectly healthy-bodied persons, who might have passed through life with scarce a thought of sickness, after being indoctrinated in it and softened by its follies and habituated to its self-surveillance, become borne down by numerous magnified symptoms and constant indications for pellets and attenuations. We have a very wealthy but very silly lady in our section, who has become so imbued with it that, besides incessantly dosing herself with pellets, she actually plies her birds with them whenever they fail to sing and her kittens when they fail to mew. Other devotees, as if to complete the absurdity, have given them to turkeys, sheep, dogs, cows, chickens, horses, geese, mules, etc.

Were some graceless wag to exchange or mix up the attenuations and globules of the different phials of sepia, natrum muriaticum, carbo vegetabilis, etc., so that each would contain specifics (!) the opposite in action from its label, homœopaths with perverted perception, squinting judgment and turgid imagination, in blissful ignorance of the fact, would doubtlessly continue to make their cures all the same. Indeed, a short while ago some Chicago physicians offered to test the value of homœopathy as follows : 100 vials of pellets were to be put up by homœopathic druggists, in parcels of 10 each—9 of the 10 vials to contain sugar pellets only, while the 10th vial was to be filled with some active (?) homœopathic drug. Each of these parcels were to be sent to some prominent homœopath, who was to use them on his patients, and designate, by the effect, what drug the 10th vial contained. No one was willing to accept the challenge!

Homœopathy has also profited, and is still profiting, wherever the English language is spoken, by an accidental misleading resemblance of the term homœ to the precious word home—" Home, sweet home."

To you as a physician the term homœopath naturally signifies a person who practises a certain exclusive and visionary system. But to many of the laity, on the contrary, the first two syllables of the word suggest that he practises a simple *home* or domestic system of medicine, and the fact that he ordinarily prepares his own globules, solutions, etc., either at his own home or at the homes of those who employ him, instead of sending prescriptions to drug-stores, as we do, adds strength to this popular error.

By fostering the error which this unfortunate resemblance creates—in some instances even anglicizing the term by dropping the *œ* and substituting *e*—and loudly terming all who practise rational medicine "Allopaths," Hahnemann's followers have materially advanced themselves with the public, and of course injured rational medicine in a corresponding degree.

This error is so natural that people often actually mistake regular physicians who supply their own medicines for homœopaths.

It is your duty, in the interest of truth and for the benefit of humanity, to make it known that the word "home" is of Saxon derivation, whereas the prefix *homœo* is derived from the Greek *homoios* (similar), and has no possible relation to hearth and home. Hahnemann seems to have built better than he intended, as far as the English-speaking people are concerned, when he styled himself a homœopathist, and not a pathhomœist, which has the same meaning.

One of the most curious of all wonders is that wisdom in law or theology, perfection in the sciences, skill in the arts, or acuteness, even brilliancy, in other departments of human knowledge, scarcely increases some people's reasoning powers a single jot in medical matters.

More than one gullible lawyer has put knotted strings around his children's necks to cure whooping cough; more than one sea-captain has carried a potato in his pocket to charm away rheumatism; more than one capitalist has vowed that pellets of tartar emetic have restored his strength; more than one clergyman has certified that this or that or the other worthless quack medicine has saved life.

How any individual can be one of the wisest of men in all else, and yet, as soon as sickness attacks him or his, become an easy, almost volunteer prey to shallow quackery and sophistical pretension whose assumptions are glaringly contrary to common sense, is a most curious psychical enigma.

Do not infer that a genuine homœopathist may not be following homœopathy conscientiously, for there never has been an absurdity in regard to religious, political or medical questions, that has not found very sincere supporters; nor that homœopathists do no good, for they do a great deal of good. But the good they do is *not* by *similars*, as has been proven by innumerable observers, but by the accompanying hygienics, dietetics, faith, expectation, good nursing, etc., which would do equally as much were the similars left out, and atoms of taffy or sawdust, or anything else substituted, to give their patients room to exercise their faith, and *nature* time and opportunity to do the work.

God help afflicted humanity were genuine homœopathy the medical man's only reliance in his struggles with disease. Think for a moment of a group of physicians entering the lazar-house depicted by Milton in *Paradise Lost*, to combat the afflictions of that protean assemblage with genuine *similia similibus*. True, while ministering to catarrhs, nervous headaches, palpitations, functional dyspepsia, tonsilitis, catarrhal croup, chorea, uncomplicated exanthemata, and slighter affections that have a strong tendency to spontaneous recovery, and in which the public cannot distinguish between cures and natural restoration, they might, with a little adroitness and the free use of adjuvants, make themselves appear like magicians ; but when they encountered maladies which, unless thwarted by the truest medicines and overcome by the stoutest weapons that are known to man, have a tendency to overwhelm and destroy their victims, they surely would feel in their hearts the inherent deficiency of their art, which had left them as powerless to combat disease as soldiers would be to meet their enemy in battle after being stripped of all their weapons.

The truth is, if a man has a sickness in which the tendency is to death, medicines given on Hahnemann's foolish plan will not, cannot avert that result; and the malady will go on from bad to worse till his sufferings are relieved by death, while some of the agents which experience and reason offer, and rational physicians accept, might control its downward and fatal course and restore him to health.

When chance brings you in contact with a genuine homœopathist, if you believe him to be a gentleman, observe all the forms of politeness toward him, and treat him exactly as you would any other gentleman, but ignore him *professionally*, and never allow yourself to fraternize with him in the management of a case. But have nothing, emphatically nothing, to do with any of the large flock of bread-and-butter fellows who, for their in-gatherings simply, masquerade as homœopaths by a display of Hahnemannic nonsense, just as ostrich-hunters assume to be ostriches by dressing in that *wise* bird's feathers.

The majority of these bogus homœopaths simulate the genuine by carrying with them awe-inspiring satchels similar to theirs, which they guard as carefully as if an additional shake of the powerful dynamizations within might still further increase their potency and cause an explosion. Carefully search the satchel and the pockets of any one of these and you will not only find the usual attenuations, triturations, tinctures and globules, and Lehrman's, Durham's, Lentz's, and Finck's high dynamizations ranging from the 800th away up to the terrific potency of an 86000th (nonsense that would not vary the ailments of a fly); but search a little further and you will find also a full, a very full supply of Wm.

R. Warner's, W. H. Schieffelin's, Sharp & Dohme's, or some other make of sugar-coated granules of morphia, quinia, arsenicum, belladonna, elaterium, colocynth, etc., which he habitually administers with as little regard for "*similia*," etc., as you do. Be not startled if you also find a hypodermic syringe and a bottle of Magendie's solution—damning witness of his lack of moral sense and of honesty, and of faith in what he professes. Respect every sincere believer in a false system, no matter how great his error, but let the finger of scorn point contemptuously at each and every graceless scamp who, as an advertisement of himself, denounces and sneers at "*old school*" remedies, meanwhile giving globules and attenuations in placebo cases only, and in all others, slyly using opium to relieve pain, chloral to induce sleep, quinia to arrest fever, and all our other prominent agents, *just as we do*, in full doses, yet crediting the good they do to homœopathy!

There is also a self-adjusting variety of quacks, who, thank heaven, are not very numerous, who chameleon-like, are all things to all men, and actually *offer to* practise any exclusive system people wish. These are not as bad as the bogus form, for they are at least frank and honest in their announcement. But what would you think of a clergyman whose love of gold and lack of scruple would allow him to vary his principles *at will* and preach *anything* you wished, whether a strictly Catholic lecture, or an ultra-Protestant discourse, an orthodox Hebrew sermon, a fiery Mohammedan philippic, or an out-and-out infidel harangue? He might believe in one or none, but he could not believe in all.

Examine the homœopathic creed closely (pages 192, 193) and carefully measure all those who claim to practise under it, of whom you have personal knowledge, and you will find but few (if any) who honestly do so. The genuine homœopath never alternates or mixes remedies, and never employs hypodermic injections, purgatives, mustard plasters, ointments, washes, liniments, injections, cauterizations or gargles. Show a decent respect for the real homœopath, but shun, as you would the plagues of Egypt, the fellows who, as the lion did the ass's skin, use the name simply as a cloak to deceive the gullible public because, just at this time, it pays to use it.

But few of the really sick who are persuaded into giving these false and one-idea systems a trial, become converts. Therefore be careful not to banter, irritate or abandon people who are trying *isms* or *pathies*, lest from combating them and forcing argument you *drive* them into these vagaries permanently. Should they even contend that the earth is three-cornered, or that homœopathic nonsense has saved their lives, or that pumpkins grow on trees, do not combat them *too fiercely.* Pride of opinion and determination not to be browbeaten into recantation, are unfortunate impulses to arouse, especially in conceited and silly people, and will certainly drive them to take sides against you.

If, in exposing any worthless system, you are careful not to denounce it with too much warmth or violence, as though prompted by envy or jealousy, and to confine your condemnation strictly to the impersonal abstract subject, showing that you speak your real sentiments from sober reason and conscientious devotion to the truth; and if, moreover, you avoid appearing anxious to excite hostility against the individuals who practise it honestly, your reasoning will have a great deal more weight with those whom you address and with the community, than under the reverse circumstances, for human nature is such that if a system or creed in medicine be false, abuse of its representatives will be one of the best ways of commending it to the public favor, and hence is what they themselves most heartily desire.

You will occasionally be called again to families who strayed in disgust from regular medicine years ago, when bleeding, etc., were fashionable, who will be surprised to learn that your therapeutics differ from those of your fathers—and that you no longer bleed, salivate, and give nauseous drugs, indiscriminately, as they supposed. If you are prudent and circumspect, most of these can be permanently reclaimed.

Although it is wrong to spend much time and labor in acquiring knowledge of what is useless when known, yet it is well to look into the principles of mesmerism, homœopathy, hydropathy, galvano-therapeutics, spiritualism, etc., to enable you to speak of them from personal knowledge, and to checkmate their representatives, who make great capital out of *knowing all about the "old school system,"* which they of course aver does not compare with the "new school" under which they practise.

Remember that it is *not* on account of their methods of medication that we object to *exclusive* systems and refuse to fraternize with their followers, but because they refuse to select remedies from all sources; assume dogmas and systems that are limited, and denounce all else.

14

Were you to announce yourself as an anti-herbalist, anti-homœopathist, anti-allopathist, anti-eclectic, or anything else calculated to produce division, antagonism, or strife, it would be unprofessional, and equally as inconsistent with the spirit of scientific medicine as the systems which you were opposing, and would abridge your usefulness and render you unworthy of professional fellowship, just as it does all others who follow limited creeds.

To limit one's practice is, of course, quite different from limiting one's creed. You have an indisputable right to limit your practice to any specialty or department of medicine you please, but as it is a self-imposed limitation of your sphere, you should take care in your signs and cards *simply* to add to your general title, the words, "Practice limited" to the eye, or to the throat, or to skin diseases, or to whatever else your specialty may be. Such an announcement is honest and professional, and claims nothing more in the way of skill than your M. D. presumes.

Never hold joint discussions or controversies before the public with Irregulars or quacks, either through the newspapers, or in any other way, no matter how false or shallow their pretences are, or how easily their weak arguments are refuted by stronger ones.

Such joint discussions and rejoinders, with the public as judge, would result in no good, but would bring your opponents into greater notice, gain for them new partisans, and give them a chance to raise false issues.

Bear in mind that we condemn no system, or discovery, ignorantly, on the principle which governs the Indian, who disbelieves in the telegraph, or on that by which Galileo was persecuted; but, on the contrary, claim that competent, earnest, fair-minded medical men, men eminent in science, all over the world, both in hospital and private practice—with the sole object of ascertaining the truth for the benefit of science and of suffering mankind—eagerly investigate and fully test all discoveries, theories and so-called systems of medicine when they arise, and the conjoined result gives us a true common-sense verdict. And it is no more necessary for every succeeding generation, with more useful things to think about, to waste the time necessary to retest every unreasonable medical vagary before rejecting it, than it is for every one to study spiritualism and the Book of Mormon before condemning them.

Homœopathy is not half so new as many suppose. Hahnemann started it in 1790, six years before Jenner vaccinated James Phipps, and the Organon was published in 1810. Now, in this long, long period, had it deserved scientific recognition or had there been anything at all in it worthy of adoption by the profession, it would surely, like vaccination, long since have been absorbed by scientific rational medicine, whereas the fact is that to-day it has almost faded out in the land of its birth, and is without a chair in any university of Europe.

It was chiefly the over-medication of former days that gave it a start. Were any one to originate such a system to-day, it would be still-born.

We of Maryland have unfortunately no medical laws, and our common laws do not enter into a consideration of the worth, or worthlessness, of various *isms, ists* and *pathies*, but recognize all kinds, even down to notorious quacks and impostors, precisely as they do the regular profession; therefore, if you ever occupy an official position under such laws, you will have to recognize certificates of death, vaccination, life insurance, etc., given by Irregulars of every shade, just as you do those of rational, honorable physicians. In a word, you will have to recognize officially every person whom the law recognizes. State medical laws that legalize everybody are impaired to a corresponding extent. Proper laws—laws that would effectually weed out abortionists, pretenders and quacks who knowingly deceive and defraud—should be enacted and rigidly enforced, instead of laws that compel those who administer them, to recognize such people, and actually to give them a respectability before the public which they could never otherwise attain.

Quackery subsists almost entirely on credulity, gullibility and ignorance, and it is your duty to expose it in every shape, and to save as many from its evils as you can. Wherever you meet it, lift its veil and show its unworthiness and the harm that it does.

Over-dosing, blood-letting, salivating, purging, etc., are now justly unpopular, and ultra-conservative, reconstructive medicines are in fashion. Almost every one is filled with the belief that he is debilitated. Say to the average patient " you are weak and need building up," and you will instantly see by his countenance that you have struck *his* keynote. So much is this the case, that many of the sick, fully impressed with this idea, will want you to treat them with tonics and stimulants, even when their condition is such that these medicines are not at all indicated.

You must learn to distinguish cases in which you can safely depend on nature, from those that nature cannot overcome, and treat each accordingly; for when you learn to recognize those that need an ounce of medicine and a grain of policy, and those that need an ounce of policy and but a grain of medicine, you will have entered upon the path of wisdom. When you have a patient who needs only a few drops of mint water, or a bread pill, for mercy's sake don't violate common sense and force upon him an infusion of gentian, or a large bottle of muriated tincture of iron and quinine, as if your chief aim were to *disgust* him. Give him nothing stronger or coarser than he needs, and leave the rest to nature. Chagrined homœopathists and their partisans will warmly assert that in doing these things you are infringing on them and working on homœopathic ground. But, although you will be catering to the popular taste and giving *very bland* medicine, you will administer according to common sense, without regard to *similia*, etc., and will be practising, not homœopathically, but rationally. Handle those homœopathically inclined, and those with highly impressible nervous systems who have treacherous stomachs, with kid gloves, and be careful to give them as little unpleasant-tasting medicine as possible. The recent great improvements in the forms and palatability of medicines offer you splendid opportunities to do this. Offend neither their eyes, their palates, nor their stomachs, and you will succeed, where neglect of these precautions will cause failure. Also give hypochondriacs, dyspeptics, and others who are fond of your attention, but not of your medicine, small, tasteless or palatable remedies, and, unless there is a real necessity for it, do not oblige anybody to take medicine before breakfast or to be aroused for the same purpose during the night. With such people make free use of the bland elixirs, the fluid extracts and the large line of sugar-coated granules of arsenious acid, corrosive sublimate, cannabis indica, nux vomica, morphia, podophyllin, strychnia, and other results of artistic elegance and chemical accuracy, now kept in every drug-store.

Never attempt to force the use of a remedy—mercury, arsenic, iodide of potassium, opium, asafœtida, valerian, etc.—on a person after he has exhibited an idiosyncrasy towards it.

The smaller, the more striking the means that seem to accomplish a result, the more surprising does that result appear to a patient. It does not seem wonderful to him that he should get better after taking an ounce or a pint dose of anything, but improvement following a tiny powder, or a pellet, or a tasteless solution, or a morphia granule, appears marvellously strange and is very pleasing.

Carry a phial of sugar-coated morphia granules with you constantly, and give a proper number of them as soon as you reach one of the thousand cases in which great pain is a symptom. By so doing you can often adroitly meet the emergency, relieve the suffering, and show your power over pain, before the messenger could get back from the drug-store with the remedy you would otherwise order.

You can also use them to give jaded sufferers an occasional night of placid slumber, or of delicious visions, even though they form no essential part of the treatment.

Morphia granules given thus make a vivid impression in the physician's favor, and do great good, becoming, in fact, almost a perfect substitute for the hypodermic syringe.

CHAPTER X.

" Behold, how good and how pleasant *it is* for brethren to dwell togethei in unity 1 "—PSALM cxxxiii. 1.

Be just and friendly towards every worthy druggist. Owing to the close relationship between pharmacy and medical practice, the pharmacists are your natural allies, and should receive your friendship and respect. Probably all physicians will agree that in the ranks of no profession can a greater proportion of gentlemen be found than in the pharmaceutical.

An excellent rule is strictly to avoid favoritism, and let all reliable druggists compete for your prescriptions and for the family patronage which they influence. You will make a serious mistake, and engender active enemies, too, if you step out of your way and without proper cause instruct patients to buy their medicines from any particular drug-store ; if a prescription is properly compounded it makes but little difference by whom, so the compounder is honorable and reliable.

Do not deter your patients from patronizing a druggist simply because he is also a graduate in medicine, unless he is uniting the two callings from mercenary motives, or habitually prescribes, or has the drug-store as a stepping-stone to get acquaintances and a practice, as a preliminary to making his debut as your antagonist or rival; but if you fold your arms and allow your prescriptions to be compounded by a drug-store physician who *prescribes* over his counter, or in the office or parlor, free of charge, and makes it up on the medicine ordered, you will, unless he shows less than the usual amount of selfishness, sooner or later regret it.

Independently of all other considerations, the practice of pharmacy and medicine simultaneously is too much for even the most intelligent of men, and one or the other is apt to be slighted; and if your prescription falls into the hands of such parties, both you and your patient must take a great many risks.

There is not the slightest wrong in having your name printed on your prescription papers. But do not use a prescription paper which has any other name upon it besides your own. If it contains the name of a druggist it will naturally suggest collusion or something else not complimentary; if it contains some enterprising fellow's commercial puff, it will indicate very ordinary taste for you to use it. It is probably better always to write on good plain paper; although it could do no harm to have some such phrase as the following printed on the back of every prescription paper, for the benefit of the public, and the protection of your own interests: "A remedy that is useful for a patient at one time, may be improper for the same patient at another time, or for other persons at any time, even though suffering with the same affection."

It would be wrong, *very wrong*, to receive from an apothecary a percentage on your prescriptions as payment for sending them to his store, and for this reason: were you to accept such an offer, it would be robbing the purse of either the apothecary or the patient. Were the former to allow you ten cents for each prescription, and reimburse himself by adding that amount to the sum charged the patient for the remedy, it could not be looked upon in any other light than that you had combined to *fleece* ten extra cents from every poor sufferer who trusted to your honor. On the other hand, if the druggist had more honesty than you and allowed you to shear ten cents from his legitimate profit, because compelled to do so or lose your influence, it would place you in a most contemptible position, and you would live in constant danger of an exposé and an indignant public sentiment that the strength of Hercules could not, and the angry God of Justice would not, arrest.

Honesty is the great keystone; without it, the whole arch of honor falls. You must live, and must have fees to enable you to do so, but unless you obtain every cent honestly and honorably you cannot escape the finger of scorn.

Watch zealously that the public do not imbibe a belief that you are a part owner of, or interested in, the drug-store which compounds the largest number of your prescriptions. If such a suspicion be expressed by any one, take care to inform him that you have no such interest.

If any druggist volunteers to supply a physician and his immediate family with medicines either free or at a nominal price, or with such proprietary articles as he needs, at cost, the favor can be conscientiously accepted, but it seems very unjust for any one to expect or allow him to supply a whole generation of uncles, aunts and cousins on similar terms.

Never supply one or several druggists with private formulæ that other druggists cannot understand, as it would at once suggest trickery. A still meaner device would be to have a private, a cheating code, for use between you and a druggist. Surely neither you nor any other honest person needs warning against such infamous systems of swindling as these, for any one who would resort to private codes, or cipher prescriptions, for money-getting is weak and unworthy, and might be very properly classed with the Shylocks who accept a percentage on prescriptions and the wretches who produce abortion.

Although the law has decided that a prescription belongs to the patient, the druggist, after compounding it, has a natural right to retain it as his voucher, but he has no right to repeat it without your consent.

The unauthorized renewal of prescriptions by druggists has often produced the opium, alcohol, chloral, and other enslaving habits. Now we all know that it is often unsafe for a person to take a medicine ordered for another, or even the same medicine at different times. Furthermore, how can the druggist conscientiously label the second quantity, "Take as directed by Dr. A.," when the physician is not even aware of the renewal?

In consequence of the present unfair habit of many druggists, the unauthorized renewals of prescriptions probably outnumber those of the authorized, five to one.

Drug-stores have become so numerous of late, and the area from which each must draw its patronage is so small, that druggists, in order to exist, have either to charge very high for the medicines prescribed, or *substi-*

tute inferior drugs; the result is that drug bills have gradually grown greater and greater, till of late they almost eclipse the expense of medical attendance. Many people, to avoid what appear to them *exorbitant* prices, actually buy quack medicines, make home mixtures, wend their way to no-drug homœopaths, or trust entirely to nature, instead of paying for prescriptions and then having to pay heavily to have them compounded.

The cost of medicines may be slightly reduced, by instructing your patient to save the cost of the bottle by carrying one *with* the prescription; doing so is not at all objectionable to druggists, as they charge only *cost price* for bottles. A good way to decrease the cost of certain prescriptions is to omit inert and unnecessary ingredients; for example, if you prescribe a mixture of wine of colchicum root, tincture of digitalis and sulphate of morphia for a patient, do not amplify what would naturally be a one-ounce mixture, that would cost about thirty-five cents, into three or four ounces by adding syrup, water, or other vehicle, thus swelling the dose to a tablespoonful and the cost to a dollar. Prescribe the necessary articles only, and let the directions tell how many drops to take and how, and when.

Another evil resulting from there being too many druggists for all to live by legitimate business, is that some, to make both ends meet, encroach on the domain of medical practice, usurp our province, and prescribe for every foolish applicant that comes along whose case does not appear to be formidable, and thus build up a large office (or store) practice. How many simple cases are in this way yearly converted into incurable ones, and how many new ailments are induced by such prescribing, heaven only knows. Fully one-half of all diseases of imprudence, biliousness, debility, cough and the like are now seen and treated by druggists, or their apprentices, before applying to physicians. Those whose complaints prove simple are, of course, cured like magic by the *four little pills* which the druggist recommends, or by the liniment he devises, or by *his great* fever-and-ague mixture, etc.; and they, thinking that some terrible spell has been turned aside, laud the druggist to the skies and advise all to go to—Doctor Pharmacist, instead of consulting a physician, with assurances that he is as good as the latter and a great deal cheaper.

Another, although lesser evil, is this: If a patient's better sense carries him in the first place to a physician for advice, instead of to a druggist, there is every probability that he who takes the prescription to be compounded, will be presented at the drug-store with one or two quack almanacs or advertising pictures, or that the bottle of medicine will be wrapped in some pushing fellow's handbill. The druggist's co-operation as retailing agent for quack medicines is indispensable to quackery; without it most of the harm that patent medicine literature is doing, would cease, the vain promises that keep the public rushing from one noisy novelty to another, would no longer entice, and at least two-thirds of the quack specifics and proprietary trash that now curse our land, would pine away and perish.

You had better avoid all druggists whose presumption leads them to assume the rôle of physician. This, of course, does *not* refer to *emergencies*, in which a druggist acts as a humanitarian. Medicines are the physician's tools; a druggist may prepare them and handle them for a lifetime and be an excellent compounder, and yet, as his studies are pharmaceutical, and not therapeutical, he may know no more about prescribing for the sick properly, than the mechanic who makes needles or scissors does about dressmaking, or the manufacturer of trowels and ploughs and chisels about bricklaying, farming or carpentering.

Be also on your guard against instrument-makers and dealers who meddle with surgical cases, and manufacturers of appliances for deformities, etc., who presume to treat cases that should be referred to the physician or surgeon; and in fact, avoid encouraging any one who encroaches on the physician's province.

Make it a point never to style a druggist, a preacher, or any one else, " Doctor," unless he *is* a doctor. Heaven knows the title is cheap enough without bestowing it on those who have not even applied for it.

Avoid over-praising prescribing druggists to your patients, or people will, on your word, overestimate them, and rely on their gratuitous advice, instead of on the physician's, at least in all moderate cases.

Beware of *indiscreet* druggists; as those who talk too freely, who converse, joke, etc., while compounding prescriptions, who put wrong directions, or the wrong physician's name on bottles, or surprise and alarm people by charging a different price every time a prescription is renewed, as if they had no system, or as if the medicines were put up wrong, who make the impression that it takes them half their time to correct the mistakes of the other half, or who in other ways show abstraction or careless compounding. For such people be especially careful how you abbreviate and how you make your ℥'s and ℈'s, and carefully dot every i and cross every t in your prescriptions.

In ordering syringes, brushes, atomizers, breast-pumps, probangs, etc., with your prescriptions, be careful to specify the kind or size you wish. To write a prescription for a solution and add, "also a syringe for using," is often as perplexing to the druggist as if you were to send for a slip of adhesive plaster as long as a string, or for a lump of rhubarb the size of a piece of chalk.

If you believe on good authority that any druggist so far forgets himself as to make disparaging comments upon you or your remedies, doses, or apparent inconsistencies, or to exhibit and decry your prescriptions to Irregulars, laymen, or other physicians, or to make unauthorized substitutions, give under-weight of expensive ingredients, or omit them altogether, or to join with our enemies in reviling our profession and its imperfections, or in nick-naming different physicians in derision, or to keep his prescription file open to miscellaneous inspection, or to have a medical protégé under his wing, to whom he endeavors to direct customers for sinister purposes, or to be guilty of any other grossly unprofessional conduct, you are justified in directing your patients to go elsewhere for medicines.

You may take the following as somewhat of a guide in determining whether this or that drug-store is worthy of confidence. Among the distinguishing features of a properly conducted drug-store are:

1. Proprietor a practical pharmacist.
2. Competent and courteous assistants.
3. Pride and skill shown in selecting and preparing pure medicines.
4. Full line of pure drugs kept.
5. Store neat and orderly.
6. Quiet and discipline maintained.   No loungers.
7. No liquors sold as beverages.
8. Not a bazaar of general merchandise.
9. Nostrums shown and sold only when called for.
10. No habitual prescribing.
11. Charges neither cheap nor exorbitant.
12. Prompt attention and accuracy characteristic.

Among the features that mark improperly conducted ones are :

1. Patent medicine signs prominently displayed.
2. Patent and proprietary remedies paraded and pushed.
3. Wines and liquors sold as beverages.
4. Engrossing attention to sale of soda water, cigars, tobacco, fancy goods, etc.
5. Indiscriminate renewals of prescriptions.
6. Habitual prescribing over the counter.
7. Disparagement of physicians to the laity.
8. Loose management of store.
9. Store a resort for political or other cliques.
10. Unchaste conversations and conduct.
11. Dealing in articles used for immoral purposes.
12. Unnecessary delay and detention of customers.

Be prompt and decided in refusing to give professional certificates to anything secret; do not be too liberal even in giving them to legitimate pharmaceuticals, and never issue one founded on any other basis than purity of ingredients, or special skill or experience in compounding them.

Willingness to give medical certificates is an almost universal weakness of mankind. The idea of being paraded in print as " an authority " dazzles all classes, and makes them willing to have their names and ailments paraded in almanacs, handbills and newspapers. Many people could almost be inveigled into certifying that in medical matters two and two make five, by any sharper who understands how to tickle their self-conceit and their love of notoriety.

Be also chary in giving (un)professional certificates to any one on disputed or partisan questions, or regarding surgical appliances, copyrighted medicines, wines, mineral waters, beef extracts, health resorts, etc., for they will affect the general professional interest, as well as yours. When you give one, persons who happen to know you, may regard its personal and not its professional significance, but every one else all over the land will notice your title only. When John Doe gives his certified opinion that ice is *hot* and fire is *cold*, it remains simply John Doe's opinion ; but when John suffixes his title of M. D., he undoubtedly gives that certificate a professional significance, and, to some extent, involves our entire profession therein.

Judge certificate-giving by its effects on our own profession. One of the worst inflictions we endure to-day is the endless parade of certificates from clergymen, politicians, merchants, lawyers and other well-known persons recommending all kinds of medical nostrums. You know, and every wise man knows, that such certificates are not worthy of credence, and that the preacher of Gospel truth who, with absurd solemnity, lends his name and the cloak of religion to assist wily charlatans and commercial sharpers to prey on the afflicted, must be either a silly dupe or a cruel knave.

Every quack knows the influence of a clergyman's endorsement, and hence makes special and often successful efforts to obtain it, feeling certain that he can easily entrap the individuals of the flock after the leader is secured, and it is a singular fact that though few men get more gratuitous service out of physicians than ministers of the Gospel, yet no class do more to injure the profession, by the countenance they give to various kinds of quackery, pathies and isms.

In signing certificates in life insurance, or beneficial societies, or in giving your name for directories, state or city registers of physicians, or in other cases in which the form requires you to state what school of medicine you practise, be careful to record yourself as a *regular* or *rational* physician, and not as an allopathist.

Whenever you are asked by proprietors or plausible drummers, or tempted by glowing advertisements, highly colored certificates, epitomized treatises on therapeutics and practice, etc., to prescribe semi-secret trade-mark pharmaceuticals, copyrighted medicines, and the various elixirs, restoratives, tonics, panaceas, and other specialties with attractive *ideal* titles, gotten up by crusading druggists, manufacturing pharmacists, pharmaceutical associations, etc., to catch the popular eye and the popular dollar—think of the cunning cuckoo (see p. 30), and how its one egg hatches evil to the whole nest, and do not use them.

To fully realize the enormous proportions of the proprietary remedy method of replacing physicians, and of the mercenary motives that lie at the bottom of it, and the injury it inflicts on health, credit and business, go and take a bird's-eye view of the vast and bewildering array of empirical and proprietary compounds which the quack and proprietary departments of any wholesale drug-store contain, and then reflect on the enormous sums of money spent in puffing them. Thus enlightened, you can hardly fail firmly to resolve henceforth no longer to immolate yourself on that altar.

Unless you have missed your profession, and if you are capable of thinking and have any ingenuity at all, the United States pharmacopœia and the dispensatory should certainly be large enough to allow you to exercise yourself freely in the art of prescribing, to think out your prescriptions and to make *any* required combination, and you should assert your intelligence and follow this, the legitimate mode of prescribing, and let ready-made substitutes for medical attendance alone.

The principle governing our condemnation of secret nostrums is this: They not only do more harm than good, but, if puffing and advertising alone are enabling the proprietor of a quack remedy to fleece the sick, its unprincipled owner deserves exposure and contempt. If the nostrum is really valuable, *which is very rarely the case*, its composition should be freely and fully disclosed for the benefit of the sick and suffering.

You should also maintain your independence and never order A's, B's or C's make of anything, *unless* you have some specific therapeutic reason for so doing. To particularize thus would not only reflect injuriously on every other manufacturer and cause a still greater popular distrust of our materia medica, but would also put the compounder to additional trouble and expense; for he might have half a dozen other varieties of the same article in his stock, and yet be compelled by your specification to get another. I knew one case in which the druggist, though he had twenty-one different preparations of cod-liver oil emulsions, had to get the twenty-second to fill such a prescription. Besides, it almost invites substitution.

Do not, however, oppose any remedial agent that is a distinct improvement in pharmacy, or any particular brand of anything on account of its being a monopoly, if that monopoly is owing to unusual skill, superior quality of medicine used, or great perfection in its manufacture.

Patients think physicians know precisely what a medicine ought to cost, and will often ask you *how much* the druggist will charge for the remedies you have prescribed. Answer promptly that you do not know, and avoid mentioning any specific sum; because, were you to guess too high, they might infer that he had either made a mistake, or used inferior drugs; and were you to guess too low, they would probably accuse the druggist of overcharging, and perhaps drag your name into their squabbles.

Whenever you prescribe a remedy that is unusually expensive, such as musk, quinia, oil of erigeron, etc., take care to inform the patient of that fact, and that expensive drugs are no more profitable to the druggist than cheaper ones, so that he will not be surprised and cavil when the druggist tells him how much he charges for it.

Notice particularly whether an apothecary gives unusual prominence to nostrums, quack almanacs and placards, or has quack advertising signs painted on his doors or outside walls, and it will give you a true insight into his aims and attitude towards our profession. If you see that he is pushing the *quack* department, with quack proprietors' portraits in his windows and hanging around his store, and his own name and influence used in handbills and almanacs as a vendor of nostrums, bitters, plasters, pads, etc., or selling liquor as a beverage, you may be sure that he is conducting his store simply as a tradesman, on a *trade basis* instead of a professional one, which supposes him to love his profession and to devote his chief attention to the inspection and preparation of pure and reliable drugs, and filling prescriptions with scrupulous exactness; and you will fulfil a moral obligation by rigidly shunning him.

Possibly you have no right to ask that the druggist should not handle quack and proprietary medicines, or anything else for which there is a demand, as he keeps his store to make a living; you have an undoubted right, however, to expect him to keep them out of sight, to be shown only when called for, just as he does sweet spirits of nitre, syrup of the iodide of iron, syrup of ipecac, and other articles, instead of pushing their sale by displaying their announcements head and shoulders above legitimate pharmaceuticals.

In drugs and medicines purity and accuracy are of the first importance, because the uniformity in action of every medicine is in proportion to its purity and goodness; some of our leading remedies vary greatly in quality and in strength, and this is one of the occasional causes of uncertainty in the practice of medicine, and such variability would modify your efforts too much to be risked in any important case. A badly compounded prescription may rob you of your reputation and deprive the patient of his chances of recovery. Therefore, if you think an important prescription is likely to be sent to a druggist whom you conscientiously believe to have inferior or unreliable articles, it is your duty to direct the messenger to go elsewhere; for, being responsible for the patient's welfare, and having your own reputation to care for, you have a perfect right, and indeed it is your duty under such circumstances, to order your remedies to be procured where you believe your prescriptions will be exactly filled. The art of medicine is imperfect enough at best, and you will encounter plenty of new and strange problems to remind you of your lack of aids and of the insufficiency of human resources, without adding the risk of being thwarted by an unreliable druggist; but when you find it necessary to *ignore* any one for this reason, take care to do so in a discreet, ethical manner, and with as little personality as possible.

You will for various reasons often wish you had synonyms for the terms quinia, zinc, opium, chloral, strychnia, morphia, and probably for other articles in daily use. Whenever a synonym for any of them is supplied, use it. By employing the terms ac. phenicum

for carbolic acid, secale cornutum for ergot, kalium for
• potassium, natrum for sodium, chinin for quinia, etc.,
you will debar the average patient from reading your
prescriptions and hampering you, which is in many cases
highly desirable. You can also further eclipse his
wisdom by transposing the terms you use from the
usual order and writing the adjective in full with the
noun abbreviated; e. g., instead of writing quiniæ
sulph., write sulphatis quin., etc., etc.

Take care to have all powerful remedies for external
use labelled "for external use," or "not to be taken,"
which will not only prevent misunderstandings, but in
case they are swallowed by mistake, it will save you
from censure; also, for the same reasons, be careful to
order all mixtures that may separate on standing, to be
shaken before pouring out the dose, otherwise the
patient may get all the active ingredients in either the
first few or the last few doses.

When you prescribe a remedy for external use, and at
the same time one that is to be swallowed, take care to
tell the patient how each will look and smell, that he
may not confound them and swallow the wrong one.
Absent-minded druggists have more than once put liniment labels on bottles containing remedies for internal
use, and those designed for the latter upon liniment
bottles, thereby leading to fatal mistakes, which a word
of explanation from the physician to the patient might
have prevented.

Druggists might easily avoid the possibility of ex-
changing labels thus, by compounding one and labelling
it before beginning the other. Directing the druggist to

put a *red* label on the bottle for external use offers some
security against mistakes.

You will notice that some druggists label the remedies they compound for you, with their *file numbers only*,
thus, 17,483 ; while others pursue the much more satisfactory plan of adding the date on which it was compounded, thus 17,483, 19-7-85, signifying that it is number 17, 483, and that it was compounded July 19th, 1885.
The latter plan will enable you to distinguish between
the dates at which you prescribed different bottles of
medicine, and otherwise be of service to you.   I am sure
the majority of druggists would cheerfully make use of
this system if they were aware how often it assists the
physician.

It is well to request neighboring pharmacists always
to inform you of any ambiguity or apparent mistake in
your prescriptions before dispensing them, and in return,
when you suspect there has been a mistake in compounding a prescription, be very careful not to make your
suspicion known by either word, look, or action, till you
have conferred with the person who compounded it.

Bear in mind that the druggist is only human, and
that he, like every other person, requires some *rest* and
relaxation, and do not order mixtures requiring tedious
manipulations, or direct filthy ointments to be mixed, or
dirty plasters to be spread, suppositories to be moulded,
or other unpleasant duties to be performed on Sunday,
or during sleeping-hours, unless they are urgently
needed.

CHAPTER XI.

"Sound policy is never at variance with substantial justice."—THAER.

As a physician you will sustain two relations to your patients : first, during sickness you will give them all your skill and employ whatever remedies will be most surely, most safely and most rapidly beneficial; to this you will add your deepest sympathy and tenderest commiseration. Later, when by recovery, or death, your skill and compassion are no longer required, you will enter upon the second, or business relation, and then you should demand and secure a just remuneration for your services.

Business is business. The practice of medicine is the work of your life; it is as honest, as useful, and as legitimate as any other; in fact, no one earns his means of living more fairly, and often more dearly, than the physician.

You are human, and must live by your avocation just as other people live by theirs, but this you cannot do unless you have a business system, for upon *system* depend, both your professional and your financial success. Neither untiring study, nor unselfish devotion as a humanitarian, can lift you above the demands of the tailor, the instrument-maker, the bookseller, the grocer, the butcher and other creditors, not one of whom will take your reputation of working for *philanthropy*, or your smiles, thanks and blessings, for his pay; nay, even the conductor will repudiate such sentimental notions, and put you off the street-car which is carrying you to your patient, if you do not have money to pay your fare with. It is, of course, a pleasant thing to be *very popular*, but even though your popularity embrace the entire city, it will neither fill your market-basket nor purchase books, pay your office rent nor buy horse feed; and though money is *not* the immediate or chief object in the practice of medicine, it ever has been and ever must be one of the ultimate objects, and no one can sustain his practice without a money feature. If people do not pay you, you cannot live by your calling, and you will very soon tire of *all work and no pay*.

The nearer your financial arrangements approach the *cash* system, the better it will be for you and your family. Frequent accounts are best for the physician. It is often more advisable even to submit to a reduction in a bill for prompt payment, than to let the account stand and run the risk of losing it through the pay-when-you-please system. After settling promptly, many patients will feel free to send for you again and make another bill, even in moderate sickness, instead of dally-ing with home remedies or quack medicines, as they might do if they still owed you.

You should present your bills while they are small, and your services are still vividly remembered, for an-other reason: 'if you are neglectful or shamefaced and do not send your bills promptly, it will create a belief that you are not dependent upon your practice for a living, have no wants and do not need money, or that you do not hold this or that person to your business rule, or are not uneasy about what *they* owe you; and if you foster such notions, a bad system will grow up around you, and great, irreparable loss will result. Asking for payment reminds patients that there is still a little of the human left in a man, even if he is a physician, and that you have to live, and must have your fees to enable you to do so.

The business of the world is now conducted on the *cash* system, instead of the old *long credit* plan, and you should do your share towards breaking up the unjust custom that physicians used to follow, of waiting six months or a year after rendering services before sending a bill. If a physician attends a person, say, in February, and sends his bill in March or April, it seems to the patient like a current expense, and as though the doctor lives by his practice, and it is apt to be paid promptly; whereas, if he delays sending it until July or January, and then sends one headed with the semi-apology, " Bills rendered January 1st and July 1st," as an excuse for even sending it then, the debtor will naturally think that the physician has merely sent it out with a whole batch of others, *more* because he has posted his books than from a special desire for its payment; and in this belief he will probably let it remain unpaid for months longer, and perhaps delay its settlement till it becomes an old back debt, which is the hardest kind to pay. Besides, time effaces details; and recollection of the number of visits, the physician's watchings, cares and anxieties are also forgotten, and the bill, though really moderate, is apt to look large. All these circumstances combined are apt to make people feel, when they do pay an old bill, not as though they are paying a well-earned fee, but more as if they are doing a generous thing and making the physician *a present* of that amount.

If, in spite of these facts, you do send your bills only every six months, instead of putting on them " Bills rendered every six months," put " Bills collected at the end of every six months."

You will have to make a great reduction in many large bills after they have become old, therefore look after them while they are small and recent. Indeed, if you let one bill be added to another till the total reaches a considerable amount, you may place it wholly beyond the power of the person to pay it, and wrong-fully *force* him into the position of a dishonest man.

The very best time to talk business and have an understanding about your fees with doubtful or strange patients is at your first visit or at the first office interview, and the best of all times to judge people's true character will be, not on occasions for social intercourse and amenities, but when you have money dealings with them. Even a single dollar will sometimes show you exactly what a person is.

Railroad and steamboat companies and other corporations, also proprietors of mills, factories, workshops, etc., whose employés get injured, in order to relieve themselves from responsibility, or from fear of incurring public odium, or from a selfish fear that they may become involved in damage suits and be made pecuniarily responsible for the injury, often send, directly or indirectly, for a physician to attend, and in one way or another create an impression in his mind that they will pay the bill, but afterwards, on one plea or another, (usually this—that they have supported the injured person during his disability, which is as much as they can afford), either entirely disown the debt or refuse to pay it, and with such excuses leave the physician in the lurch.

In such cases, you can obviate this result and secure justice, or at least ascertain the prospect, by going, as soon as possible after you have taken charge, directly to head-quarters, or to whoever has the right to make the company or firm financially responsible for your services, and after explaining the labor and responsibility which the case involves, make known your fear of not being recompensed for your services unless they will see to it, and frankly ask if they will assume the responsibility.

From similar motives, the financial heads of families, for their own satisfaction, for social reasons, or from a feeling of insecurity lest some inmate of their house who has become sick, has a contagious disease, will sometimes have you visit their servants, nurses or poor relatives, and then escape payment of your bill on one pretext or another. These cases should be approached in a similar manner as in the last instance.

Make it a rule to enter the names of those who are financially responsible for such services in your book, and keep a memorandum of the facts that make them so, and make out your bill to them accordingly.

If you take these precautions, it will prevent many unpleasant misunderstandings and save you many a hard-earned dollar.

Make it a rule never to accept a commission or fee from any one under circumstances which you would not *willingly* submit to investigation by the public, a medical society, or a court of justice. Your severest test will be when money is enticingly offered to induce you to do doubtful things.

You will not have practised long before you will find that your welfare will not depend upon how much you book, but upon how much you collect, and that if you never insist upon the payment of your fees, you can never separate the chaff from the wheat. If you have a rule and people know it, they associate you and your rule together. Let the public know what your system is in the early years of your practice, or you cannot do so afterwards. When a new family employs you, render your bill as soon after the services as gentility will allow, especially if there has been a previous attendant who was an indifferent collector or no collector at all. Send your bill as a test, and if there is objection to you because you want your fee, the sooner you find each other out and have an understanding, or part company, the better it will be for you.

When patients ask you how much their bills are, or how much they owe you, after office consultations, operations, etc., always answer promptly, soberly and decidedly, " one dollar " or " ten dollars," or whatever else the amount is. If you avoid preceding, or following this reply with any other words, most people will in the embarrassment of the moment, proceed to pay you without objection, whereas if you add more words, it will weaken your claim in their minds, or make them believe you have no fixed charge, and will furnish them with a pretext to show surprise and to begin to contend for a reduction. When one does demur at your charge, show your amazement at his doing so, and be ready instantly to defend, or explain the justice of the charge.

Accounts for surgical cases, midwifery, poisoning, and, in fact, for all unusual cases, should be promptly "charged up" on your books; for unless this is attended to, the patient may come unexpectedly to pay his bill, and you may through embarrassment, or lack of full remembrance of the services, name entirely too low a figure and do yourself an injustice. Besides, having the amount already determined upon and written down shows it to be the *fixed* price, and the patient is less apt to ask for a *great* reduction, if any.

Take your fees whenever tendered. Patients will often ask, "Doctor, when shall I pay you?" or "Shall I pay you now?" A good plan is to answer promptly, "Well, I take money whenever I can get it; if you have it, you may pay it now, as it will leave no bones to pick," or "Short payments make long friends," or "Prompt pay is double pay, and causes the physician to think more of his patient," or something of that sort. Never give such answers as, "Oh, any time will do!" or "It makes no difference when," or you will soon find it to be expensive modesty.

Never neglect to post your account books; for it would be violating the first law of nature to attend faithfully to the department of your occupation that concerns others and neglect the one that concerns yourself. The Scripture command is, "Love your neighbor *as* yourself"; it does not say, Love him *more*, but it does say, The one who does not provide for his own household is worse than an infidel.

A good plan is to put the names of transient patients on your cash book, instead of blurring your ledger with them, and give a page in the latter only to patients with whom you think it likely you will have a permanent account.

When a transient patient pays cash at the visits, so as to make it unnecessary to transfer his account from your visiting list to your ledger, the simplest way to mark it paid is to turn each visit mark into a P, signifying *paid*.

You can fix your visiting list in a few moments, so that it will always open at the page then in use. To do this, clip off about half an inch of the upper corner of its front cover, thus ◣ , and then in the same way clip off the corners of the leaves thereby exposed, down to the page corresponding with the date of the act. When thus prepared, if you place your right thumb on the exposed corner of the uncut leaves, the book must open at the proper page. As time passes, clip each page when you wish to pass from it.

Your visits and cash entries in your visiting-list and day-book should be written in ink; for being original entries, they would be accepted in court as legal evidence. A good way to prevent forgetting any one or anything is to put names, visits, etc., down in your visiting-list with a lead pencil without delay, till you have a chance to rewrite them with ink.

At the end of every week add up the visits made to each one whom you have attended during the week, and after ascertaining the total sum which you should charge therefor, put that amount on the visiting-list in the blank spaces found at the end of the lines after the Saturday column. By doing this weekly, you can accurately estimate and charge the value of your services to each patient, while they are still fresh in your mind. It is wise not only to enter at the end of each week the amounts charged, but also to write the names of the members of the family who have been under your care during the week, in the visiting-list over the visits, *for reference*, in case your attendance should ever be disputed.

In posting your account books at the end of each month, in order to avoid missing any entry in transferring your visiting-list charges to the ledger, use a regular checking-off plan. A very good way is to make a list of the names of all patients whom you have treated during the month, on a sheet of foolscap paper; then bring from the visiting-list to the foolscap the amounts marked for each week's services and put them after their respective names; after you have all the charges transferred in this way to the foolscap, run over your ledger, page after page, and look at every account as you go along. When you reach the name of any one against whom you have a charge to make, add up all you have marked against him and enter the total on his page of the ledger; but, instead of wasting time to write November, 1885, $7.00, enter it 11–85, $7.00, then cross that person's name off the foolscap list, and continue on, page after page, through the entire ledger. By this crossing-off system, if you fail to charge any one's account as you

16

pass it, it will remain *uncrossed* when you get through the list, and will thus be detected. While going over the different pages of the ledger to enter charges, notice all accounts that need *rendering*, and take the number of each one's page on one of a pile of blank bills at hand for the purpose (or on a slip of paper), so as to *return* and make out his bill after completing all your entries; also make, while turning the pages, a list of such delinquents as it would be proper for you, or your collector, to ask for money during the approaching month.

When you make out a bill, put on your ledger, in the space just after the amount, *the date* on which the bill for that amount was rendered; thus, $7.00, with 1–8–85 after it, would signify that a bill for seven dollars was rendered to that person on the first day of the eighth month, 1885, or it may be written as the Quakers do, month first, then day, and then year, thus: 8–1–85. (Enter payments in a similar way.)

A good way to save the trouble of looking over worthless or dead accounts on your ledger, month after month and year after year, is to cross them off, using lead pencil, which can be erased at any time, if necessary, for such as may possibly be revived; and for those that are dead, or sure, from other causes, never to employ you again, use ink.

That a patient whose name is on your books is a colored person, can be easily indicated by putting three dots after his name, thus: Robinson, John ⫶ 13 Columbia street.

Patients will occasionally dispute the correctness or justice of your charges. If a bill is not correct, correct it cheerfully; if it is correct and just, do not allow yourself to be browbeaten into the position that it is not. Many people are not aware that the charges for *surgical* and various *extra* cases are higher than ordinary visits; some seem to think that for a visit at which you reduce a dislocation, open a large abscess, make a vaginal examination, or draw off the urine, you should charge the same as for ordinary visits; others have an idea that physicians do not, or should not, charge for every visit when they make more than one visit in a day, or for every patient when more than one in a house is sick. Of course, you must correct their error by explaining the difference, or, if necessary, by reference to the fee table.

Never undercharge for your services. It is ruinous to your interests and the interests of the entire profession. The tendency of undercharging is to depress the fee table permanently and to compel all physicians to work for under-pay. There is a vast difference between underbidding in our profession and underbidding in ordinary business pursuits. In the latter, cut-rates are only temporary; for, if merchants were to sell goods at or below cost for a length of time, failure would result. In business wars one withdraws, or they compromise and each advances again to full prices; warring physicians, on the contrary, having no goods to manufacture or to sell, can keep up the strain of rivalry for years, give their skill to everybody for insignificant or nominal fees, impoverish one another, and almost starve those depending on them for support.

The wisest rule in charging for your services is to ask from the beginning of your career the fees usual for the best attendance, neither extravagantly high nor ridiculously low.

Let people know that you strive to make your bills as small as possible, not by undercharging, but by getting them well with as few visits as possible.

Never bargain to attend a patient or a family by the year; it is better to be paid for exactly what you do, than to have some people feel that they are giving you twenty dollars for five dollars' worth of service, and to feel that you are giving other people fifty dollars' worth of service for twenty dollars.

Also, never bargain to attend whole neighborhoods of poor people at reduced rates; it is lowering and never works successfully. Indeed, if you ever attend a confinement or other case in a family for a nominal fee, you will not be able to raise the fee to the regular price again in that family, or even with others who hear of it.

Even though you are sure you will have to receipt your bill for a reduced amount, make it out for the standard sum, that the debtor may know your rates, and give you proper credit for whatever reduction you make; in other words, when you make a reduction to those who plead poverty or other acceptable reason, let them understand that you are not reducing your charges, but are taking something *off* their bill, and enjoin upon them not to tell it around, lest it injure your scale of charges elsewhere.

When people talk to you about taking off part of their bill because they are poor, and making the rich pay you more to make it up, take less if you think proper, but say not a word that would allow them to infer that you, or any other physician, would charge any one, whether rich or poor, a cent more than *he* honestly owes.

It is customary and just to charge *double* for the first visit to a case, chiefly for the following reasons: You must at the first visit devote an extra amount of time and attention to learning the history of the case—must involve yourself in a diagnosis, and probably also in a prognosis,—must establish a line of treatment,—must instruct the nurses,—must map out the diet, point out the requirements of hygiene, lay down rules regarding temperature and ventilation, and formally assume all the responsibilities of the case. These combined fully justify a double charge for the first visit.

There are a few people who think that when a case is severe enough to require the physician to make more than one visit a day, he should not charge for the additional visits, unconscious, as it were, of the fact that cases dangerous enough to require an extra number of visits are the very ones which throw upon him the greatest responsibility, cause him most anxiety, and contribute most largely towards making his life one of hardship and self-denial.

You will often have people to complain that their bill is high and ask you to make a reduction; yet, many of these very people would not employ you, if you were a third-rate or low-priced physician. Everybody wants first-class services, but wants them as cheaply as possible. It is not human nature to prefer a fifty-cent silk to a two-dollar silk; but if people are lucky enough to get the two-dollar silk for one dollar, they congratulate themselves. They reason the same way about physicians; very few prefer or appreciate a low-priced physician.

In *unusually* severe cases, in those that require very great exposure or *extraordinary* legal or professional responsibility, in cases of restoration after poisoning or apparent drowning, in small-pox and other contagious affections, the fear of which prevents other patients, who know you are attending them, from employing you, or which compel you to lose time in changing your clothes and otherwise disinfecting yourself before visiting others not affected, or in which you have shown extraordinary skill, or had very great luck in bad cases of any kind, you should charge round fees.

It is certainly worth more to attend a person through a pneumonia which causes the physician great anxiety and necessitates much study, than one with a sore finger or toe, even though the two cases require an equal amount of time or the same number of visits.

In some cases your charge will be not so much for doing the work as for knowing how to do it; for instance, you may charge twenty dollars for the few minutes' work of reducing a luxated humerus; were this itemized it might read : " For reducing dislocated shoulder, five dollars ; for knowing how to do it, fifteen dollars."

Attendance on an only child, an eminent or very important member of the community, or a stranger who has journeyed far with an important case that requires special attention, justifies a special charge, whether attended at your office or at the homes of the patients.

In such cases be careful to pay no unnecessary visits ; for in a very important case actually requiring three visits, to which you make but three visits, they will appreciate you more highly and will more cheerfully pay a hundred dollars, than if you had also paid five additional, apparently unnecessary, visits and charged but $80 for all.

On the same principle, when you have severe cases of any kind requiring numerous daily visits, take care to diminish them markedly as soon as the necessity is over.

In extra and complex cases and where the results are apt to be grave and far-reaching, or in which you go a long distance, or at very unusual hours, or go through storms or dangers, the charge should be, not by the visit, but for the case.

Patients will often express surprise at your asking the same fee for an office advice as for a visit to their house; explain to them that although the charge is the same, it is much cheaper to be an office patient than to be visited at home, because an office patient usually comes but *once*, or *only* when his medicines are out, or when some important change has taken place in his ailment, and quits entirely as soon as possible; whereas, if you have him under care at home, your responsibility and feeling of uncertainty compel you to visit him frequently to ascertain whether he is getting along as expected. For these reasons a few office consultations with the responsibility of attending faithfully resting on the patient, if on either, often suffice, instead of many house visits, and in this way office advice becomes very much cheaper.

Many people who are mean about paying will want you to deduct largely from their bills, when these happen to be chiefly for office consultations, vaccinations and other services of the simpler kind. They should be met with the argument that if they pay you less than the average for the minor services, they must pay you more than the average for more important ones.

The difference between words used with office patients will sometimes be to you the difference between a fee and no fee. Some who consult you, if asked to call again *to let you see how they are getting along*, will, on returning, show by every word and every action that they do not expect to pay for calling, as they merely called because you requested them to do so. Therefore, unless you intend to omit the charge, it is better to *advise them to consult you again*, at whatever time you see proper to designate. This will convey an understanding that your regular fee will be charged.

When a stranger, whose honesty you have reason to doubt, consults you at your office, and instead of paying the fee postpones it, with a promise to call again, if you ask his name and residence and book them before his eyes, you will greatly increase your chances of getting paid.

Never agree to attend any one for a " contingent fee," that is, do not take patients with chronic sores, constitutional headaches, epilepsy, cancer, post-nasal catarrh, piles, dyspepsia and other chronic affections, or cases of syphilis, gonorrhœa, etc., on the "*no cure, no pay*" plan, or to pay "*if their expectations are realized*," or "*when all is over*." Make no such agreements ; for they are never satisfactory, and will generally end in your being swindled, and it may be, charged with malpractice. Use the argument that you are willing to undertake the duty, but that you *charge for services, not for results,* and must be paid for your attendance even though the patient dies, and that all who employ you *must* take the probabilities of cure or relief. You might also hint to those who you think are unworthy of credit that if they pay as they go it will encourage you, interest you more in the case, and naturally stimulate you to do your best.

Some persons suffering with constitutional syphilis, ulcerated legs, chronic eczema, etc., in which the treatment may extend through months or years, may imagine you should wait for your fees till done attending. Do no such foolish thing, as such a case may die or move away, or abandon treatment, or slip from you to another, or even resist all your attempts to cure, and you may get nothing for all your work.

It is far more just and wise in such cases to render your bills at the proper time—"for the three months ending—," or at the very furthest the first of every July and January. If they demur (which they cannot justly do), express your surprise at their doing so, and remind them that you must live by your practice, and tell them of your entire unwillingness or inability to let your fees accumulate as they suggest.

You should ordinarily manifest no undue anxiety about your fees, and make no mention of your intended charges, unless you are dealing with people notoriously unworthy of confidence, or when there is great danger of a misunderstanding, but you should not fail to demand your fee *in advance* for attending cases of *secret* diseases. If you do not, your patient will almost surely leave you about the time the case is completed, with his bill unpaid; and if you bother him about it, he will either pay it grudgingly or not at all, and if you dun him for it, will meanly assert that it was not a disease but only a strain, or that you did him no good, or almost killed him, or tell some other lie as an excuse for deserting and cheating you. Another reason why it is proper to get your fee in advance is that many would never come and pay it till you had sent them a bill by your collector, and would then indignantly claim that you had insulted and exposed them by sending a bill of that kind.

You have no right, either legal or moral, to expose the nature of any one's disease because he has failed to pay your fees.

Venereal diseases are the result generally, not of misfortune, as other inflictions are, but of imprudence, and are self-inflicted. And for this reason venereal patients have not the claim upon your sympathy of other patients. Get a just fee in all cases of this kind before you begin treatment; then stick to the patient until he is cured. He is not likely to change from you to another after he has paid you, and if his case proceeds slowly he cannot then suspect that you are purposely running a big bill on him, or delaying the cure on account of his being a good-pay patient, as he might do if he were paying you a dollar or two a visit.

Most men think they cannot have constitutional syphilis unless they have detected a terrible chancre at the beginning. You will often have difficulty in making persons who have not detected a primary sore, believe their ailment is syphilis. Some men will actually scan you and quiz you when you tell them they have the p–x, as if they thought you a quack or an impostor, trying to scare money out of them. If you can show such a patient a fac-simile of his chancre, roseola or mucous patches in your illustrated text-books on venereal diseases, or even read to him a description of them, it will awaken him to his actual condition and guard him against either neglecting his case or infecting others.

When you are certain that your diagnosis of syphilis is correct, look the patient in the eye, and with a manner that shows you speak from knowledge, tell him that in your opinion he has genuine syphilis, and be careful not to be browbeaten into taking charge of the case for a trifling fee. It is a grave disease, and the responsibility and worry of the medical attendant are often very great and very protracted; therefore the fee should *never* be nominal.

You can broach the fee question to any patient with a private disease by remarking immediately after making your first examination, " Well, I see what your case is, and am willing to take charge of it and give you my best services, *if my terms will suit you.*" This will compel him to ask you what your terms are, and will give you an opportunity to tell him. Or, if you regard the services which will be required as very valuable, whilst it is apparent that he thinks the reverse, if you will begin with the remark, " Ah! I fear I would charge you more than you would be willing to pay," this also will compel him to question you upon the subject, and that too in a somewhat more favorable frame of mind for your purpose.

Some people believe the law compels you to attend any one who chooses to send for you. *It does not;* but public opinion would justly condemn you, if you were simply, on account of fees, to refuse to attend an urgent case where humanity should prompt you to go. If you are "*too busy*" or "*not well enough,*" or have another duty to perform equally as urgent, this will generally prove sufficient to protect you against argument or criticism. But "*I'm just at dinner,*" "*I'm too tired,*" or "*I need sleep,*" or "*I am afraid I will be dragged into court as a witness,*" etc., are not accepted by the public as sufficient reasons for refusing to go to a case, and should never be offered.

Not only should you send your bill to a patient at the proper time, but if you do not hear from him within a reasonable while thereafter, emphasize it by sending another, for he may not have received the first, or may have thrown it aside, or may be neglecting it in the hope that you will let it sleep till it is forgotten or out of date.

A very *effective* plan to use with a certain slow class of patients, when you are in need of money, is to learn the date at which you will have a note or bill to pay, or when you will have to raise money for any other special purpose, and to write about two weeks before that period and inform them briefly that you will have a *special* need for money at the time you name, and ask them to come and pay you on or before that date. Most worthy people will exert themselves to comply. You can in this way approach both your best and your worst patients, and some that you cannot successfully approach for money in any other way. Asking in this way, moreover, shows that you do not want simply to get it out of their hands into yours, but that you ask for it because you happen to need it.

Another plan, good to pursue with those who habitually throw bills aside and neglect to pay them, is to send their bills some day when you are in need of funds, with a brief note asking them to pay that day, and tell your urgent reasons for asking. Even though they pay you nothing then, knowing that they have disappointed you in your emergency will make them feel impelled to pay you something the next time they call on you for services.

By letting your prompt-paying patients know in some way or other at the visit preceding the final one, that your next visit will be the last, it will serve as a gentle hint and give them time to prepare, and will greatly increase your chances of getting your bill paid *cash* at the last visit. Convalescents from severe cases who are told to visit you at your office after they are again able to walk out, in order to let you see how they are getting along, are very apt to broach the subject of settling, and either pay, or make some definite promise before leaving.

It is wise to post your books, make out bills, settle with your collector, and in fact to conduct all the features of your pecuniary department, as much out of public sight as possible, that the public may know little or nothing about you except as a medical attendant.

You cannot put all kinds of bills on the same footing; there is *one* class of patients whose bills had better be sent by mail, *another* to whom they had better be taken by your collector, *another* where you had better deliver them yourself, and *a few* prompt-pay patients with whom it is preferable to wait till they ask for them. Try to gain as much benefit as possible from a study of this fact.

Items and details had better never be specified on a bill, unless specially asked for. They often dissatisfy people, and lead to criticisms and disputes that would not arise did not the items furnish a pretext. Assume the position that those who confide in you sufficiently to put their lives and their secrets in your keeping, should feel sufficient confidence and gratitude to permit you to say what value you place on your services to them. A physician's bill that gives the *items* is apt to be disputed, or criticized, unless it is unjustly small. Bills that simply state the *total* amount, or amount due for services since date of last bill, are much more likely to be paid without dispute. The items of every bill should, however, be carefully kept on your book, that the charges may be verified if requisite.

It is well to insist on giving receipts to people when they pay you money, even though they should deem it unnecessary. Compelling every one who pays to take a receipt, not only prevents subsequent disputes, but also assists in keeping up a regular business form between you.

Avoid avarice in its various forms, meanness, oppression, cruelty, etc. If you were to shave too closely in money matters, or to be unreasonable, or too vigorous in your efforts to collect bills from any one, it would not only be wrong, but would be very apt to injure your reputation and create a hostility that time could not blot out.

For the same reason it is, as a rule, better not to charge for certificates of sickness furnished patients to enable them to draw benefits from beneficial societies, or for certificates of vaccination, etc. These are personal favors, differing from cases in which a fee is proper.

It will seldom pay you to sue people, even if you should gain the case. It is unwise for you or any other physician to begin litigation except under very aggravating circumstances, or to maintain your reputation or self-respect. You should never sue any one whose failure to pay is due to honest poverty. Be willing to do your share of charity for the virtuous poor at all times, but the necessity of earning a living should make you careful not to let that kind crowd out your pay practice.

It will usually be wiser not to send a bill for going to cases of sudden death, drowning, suicide, persons found dead, murder, etc., in which the victim is dead before you reach him, or in emergency calls, where another physician reaches the patient and takes charge before you arrive, or in other cases where your services and efforts are not called into action, or are brief or nominal or clearly useless, as a bill under such circumstances is generally not only not paid, but is harshly criticized. If, however, grateful people volunteer to pay you for your trouble, *take* whatever is right.

In hopeless cases of cancer, phthisis, etc., which, after

going the rounds of the profession, consult you in the very last stages, merely to see whether you can possibly do anything for them, you had better frankly acknowledge that you can do but little, or nothing, and decline the fee *even if tendered.*

It is usually better to make *no charge* for ordinary or trifling advice incidentally given to patients when they call to pay their bill, or to persons for whom you happen to prescribe in public places, where you are *not* pursuing your functions as a physician. Such exactions would, to say the least, risk unpleasant remembrance and harsh criticism. Every physician sometimes writes prescriptions under circumstances where, even though he be technically entitled to compensation, *his own* interests forbid his making a charge, or even accepting a fee when tendered.

Never make a charge where the fee would come from another physician's pocket; every physician attends his professional brethren and their families gratis. Some also attend clergymen and their families without charge, especially those with whom they have church relations, and those who receive salaries so meagre as to make the payment of medical fees a hardship. Where a clergyman is in the receipt of a liberal salary and his calls on you are frequent or onerous, I know of nothing in ethics to forbid your accepting from him a fee voluntarily tendered. Many of our best physicians make it a rule to charge half fees to their own spiritual advisers; that is, they make out the bills for the full amount and receipt them upon payment of half the sum.

Never oppress any one by exorbitant fees. Be especially

fair in your charges against estates, and in all other cases where unusual circumstances place the debtor at your mercy. These opportunities will truly test your honesty. When you are in doubt what to charge, look around you, then upwards, then make out your bill at such figures as will show clean hands and a clear conscience.

When you and a professional brother do each a portion of the work in cases of accident, confinement, etc., a very fair plan is to agree to charge a joint fee and divide it. When you receive such a joint fee, go at once and with straightforward manner divide every dollar with your fellow-worker, on whatever basis you have agreed upon.

Never acknowledge or work under the fee-table of any association or company, *unless* it be in harmony with the regular professional fee-table of your community.

Humanity requires you to go to all cases of sudden emergency, accidents, etc., in which the life or limb of a fellow-being is in jeopardy, without regard to the prospect, or non-prospect of a fee. You should do various things for the sake of charity; among these is to give relief to any one injured, or in great pain or distress, regardless of fees. At such times think only of your duty to humanity. The good Samaritan succored the wounded man, and took him to an inn and provided for his immediate necessities. You, as a physician, should, for humanity's sake, go and bind up wounds, mitigate pains and relieve suffering in all cases of emergency. After this is done, further attendance is, of course, optional.

17

When another physician is called to a case of yours, during your absence, not only thank him when you meet, but also insist on his sending his bill for whatever services he has rendered. No one can be expected to work under such circumstances without fee. His kindness to you consists in having responded to the call.

It is your duty to raise your voice in the profession against the encroachments of the free special dispensaries, and low fee hospitals and infirmaries which, under the great plea of *charity*, attract swarms of patients—among whom are many who are *abundantly able to pay* for medical services.

No member of the profession—and the same may be said of pharmacists and physicians who keep drug-stores and prescribe over their counters—has a right to give professional services to the public without fee, except to the moneyless poor (to whom they should be given as freely as the air they breathe); for even though there may be no loss thereby to him personally, it is taking bread from the mouths of others, and to that extent it is robbing the profession at large of its just fees.

Thousands of dependent physicians have been, of late, cheated out of their living by so-called " *Special* " Charities, carried on chiefly in the interest of individuals, or coteries, who, to foster reputation in their specialties, treat *everybody* that applies, the rich, the poor and the intermediate class, without the slightest regard to the interest of other medical men. The ultimate result of this state of things will be either that the profession will, in self-defence, be compelled to organize *self-pre-*

servation associations, or that individual physicians will take up the case and refuse to consult with any specialist, professor or surgeon who continues to render gratuitous service to those who are able to pay for it.

Never slight the worthy poor who are under the iron heel of poverty and need medical attendance; to the poor, life and health are everything, and there are none so poor but that they may amply repay your services by genuine, lasting gratitude.

Physicians render more unpaid services than any other class of people in the world. " The poor," said Boerhaave, " are my best patients. God will be their paymaster." But even in doing charity, you must discriminate. There seem to be three classes of the poor: The Lord's poor, the devil's poor, and the poor devils. The first and last are worthy objects of every physician's attention, and you should lose no opportunity to give relief to their distress. The less you have to do with the other class, *the devil's poor*, the better for you, but you will be compelled to attend more than you choose of the lowest and meanest of these, some for God's sake, and some on account of their relationship to better patients.

" Prompt payments fully appreciated," is a very useful maxim to have printed on your bills; it is truthful, and gives thanks to those who pay promptly. To those who do not, it serves as a neat admonition.

You will find that honesty and dishonesty are not confined to any one nationality, or to any station in life; but that there are many very good men and many very bad ones alike among the rich and poor, the white and black.

You will mount many a marble step, pull many a silver door-bell, and walk over many a velvet carpet for patients who will prove fraudulent in the superlative degree, and you will get many an honest fee from some who make no great pretensions and possess but little save their honesty. Indeed, the demands of fashion are now so great that many people with moderate incomes, anxious to appear better off than they really are, habitually slight their physicians in order to help keep up appearances. You will see many a man bowed down with debt and despondency, while his wife and daughters flutter around as fine as peacocks, owing everybody and paying nobody. Indeed, tricky, double-dealing women will sometimes actually intercept your bills and make it impossible for you to ask their husbands for money, unless you resort to strategy and get your bills delivered by your messenger directly to the latter ; and will even then do everything they can to postpone or entirely prevent payment.

Families will occasionally conceal from the person who is to pay your bill, the true amount of services you have rendered or the full number of visits you have paid, and thereby lead him to think you have charged very high or even overcharged for the services. Be ready promptly to correct such errors.

The most unsatisfactory and the most troublesome kind of patients physicians have to contend with are the *unprincipled tricksters* who cheat everybody that gives them a chance, and consider it no wrong at all to swindle physicians. You will be fortunate if you have tact enough to escape having anything to do with those whom you know to belong to this class. It is better mildly but firmly to decline to take patients who can but will not pay, without assigning any reason except *"too busy,"* or *"you had better get some one else,"* than to have to contend with them about your fee after your work is done, and maybe, after all, be swindled.

Tell habitual delinquents, and those who have plenty of money to buy beer, or to furnish their houses like palaces, or to follow the follies of fashion, but *none* to pay the physician—when they come to make their bills larger—that they are already as largely indebted to you as you can afford to let them be, but that you are perfectly willing to go and serve them again, *after* they pay you what they already owe you, or a reasonable part of it. This attitude will bring them to some action, or at least indicate to you the probable prospect.

You will encounter many a person who, although quite amiable during your attendance, will prove very different when your bill is presented. Allow no ground for finding fault with your manner of presenting it. It is a useful precaution to enclose bills sent by mail or messenger in a half-sheet of paper, to prevent prying custodians from peering through the envelope and recognizing its contents.

When possible, have the bills presented directly to the financially-responsible party, or the real head of the family, and say nothing at all about them to the other members of the household.

A moderately successful practitioner has about two thousand persons who call him *their* physician; whenever any one of these has a mental or physical ailment,

he must share it.   He must be bold as a lion with one
patient and as gentle as a lamb with the next.   He must
combine all good qualities and appear the perfection of
each to all men, and heaven knows! he deserves far
better treatment and a much more comfortable support
than he receives.

The fact that a physician must keep up appearances,
and that many make their visits with gloved hands, and
in stylish carriages, is regarded by many unreasoning
persons as evidence that ours is a path of ease—that we
ride around during bank hours, prescribe for a few select
patients, receive dollars by wholesale, and soon get rich,
which is a great, a very great mistake.   On the contrary,
every older physician knows that it is almost impossible
to get rich by the practice of medicine, unless it be
through a money-making specialty, commanding fancy
fees.

The truth is, when many a physician dies, those dependent on him are left poor and helpless, unless
he has acquired money otherwise than by practice.
Were you to practice for thirty years without losing a
single day, and collect eight dollars every day of your
life, you would receive but $87,600.   Deduct from that
amount your expenses for yourself and your family,
your horses, your carriages, your books, your instruments, your taxes, and a multitude of other items, for
the whole thirty years, and then, so far from being
rich, even after so long and lucky a career in this important and honorable profession—after a whole lifetime
of anxiety, responsibility and usefulness—you would
have but little, very little, left to support you in your
old age.

The physician is, as a rule, so poor a business man that if he collects money enough to meet his necessities, he is not troubled about the balance. The author had a friend, an excellent physician, who was so neglectful of his fees that he kept no systematic accounts whatever; the result was that his easy terms, together with his skill, made him unusually popular and kept him over-worked day and night till, at the end of fourteen years, the strain broke him down and he died, almost, as it were, by suicide, leaving his widow and children nothing, except regret at his foolish lack of business system. What sane physician would follow such an example!

A good, honest collector, one who has proper discretion and tact enough to get money from dilatory debtors without irritating them and making you active enemies, will be very useful, and is quite necessary if you have no time or are a poor collector yourself. Having only business transactions with patients, his interviews with them are *business exclusively,* and he can persevere in his efforts to collect, to a degree which you would find unpleasant or humiliating. Many really honest people are too poor to pay large debts, and were you to allow what they owe you to accumulate from time to time into a large bill, they could not pay it to you even if they wished, and you would actually place them in a dilemma. Having a collector prevents this, and keeps your financial department in a good condition. It also stimulates those who are habitually slow in paying, and sifts out the fraudulent before they run their bills very high.

You should have some specific agreement with your collector, not only regarding his rate of percentage for collecting, but also regarding the conditions under which he is to claim it. Among other things, stipulate that he is to make full returns to you at least once a week, that he is to have no percentage on money paid to you by those whom he has not visited for thirty days, unless you have at their request stopped him from going; and that he is to receive nothing on bills placed in his hands if the parties come and pay them before he has delivered their bills; in fact nothing on any bill which he does not in some way assist in collecting.

If you adopt some special shade or color for your bills, it will not only make them easy to find when patients mingle them with others, but will also remind those who are remiss or tardy in paying, of the debt, every time the color arrests their attention, and may, by constantly reminding them, actually secure or accelerate payment.

An interchange of lists (black-lists) of the names of fraudulent patients among physicians practising in the same section, is mutually profitable, as it often prevents the unprincipled who could pay if they wished, from systematically imposing on a succession of physicians, and coerces them into retaining and paying some one. Of course, the worthy poor, if unable to pay, should always be omitted from these lists.

CHAPTER XII.

"The physician must, like the diplomatist, tread softly."—MACNESS.

Never exhibit surprise at any possible event growing out of sickness. You will be supposed to foreknow all conceivable things relating to disease, its dangers and its terminations. Even when death has occurred to some one under your treatment unexpectedly, do not let your manner or language indicate that you were entirely ignorant of its possibility or that you consider yourself to blame.

When you have cases in which there is danger of rapid or sudden death, beware of ordering chloral, opiates, or other potent drugs in such a manner as to create a belief that they have caused or hastened death. Circumstances may even make it wise at times, not to write any prescription at all, but simply to order this or that remedy under its common name, that, its harmless nature and appropriate character being understood by all, you may not be unjustly charged with doing harm.

When any one under your treatment dies unexpectedly or mysteriously, or shortly after the use of some new means that you have directed, or after beginning some new remedy, or shortly after you have performed some operation, or just after you have pronounced him better, or in any other way that could possibly expose you to unjust censure, it is better bravely to visit his remains without delay, so as to learn about the death, to discover what attitude the friends assume towards you, and to meet their criticisms by explanations, etc. On such occasions be self-possessed, and, if need be, explain and defend your course and your treatment. By doing this you can anticipate evil reports and suppress, or shape them, before they are extensively circulated.

When you are called to a case of sudden death, the utmost composure of mind and manner is of great importance; use discretion and prudent reserve, and never assume an oracular or prophetic air, or express any opinion of the cause in any such case, until you have calmly and coolly collected and weighed all the circumstances. The possibility of death being due to disease of the heart, or brain, to poison, violence or suicide, should be carefully weighed before you express any opinion. If you neglect this precaution, further developments in the case may expose you to strong censure and deep mortification.

If you are called to a case of sudden death where violence is suspected, or to which you are summoned by the coroner, be careful to note everything connected with the corpse and its surroundings, and, where a post-mortem is required, the condition of the viscera, every one of which should be carefully examined before giving an opinion as to the cause of death. Your notes should be taken by yourself or an assistant at the time, stating the year, day of the month and hour, and should be in non-technical language, enumerating first the facts of the case, and then giving your comments and interpretation of them. These notes should be preserved, as you will be allowed to read them in court, if called there, in order to *refresh* your memory, though not wholly to rely on them. If the cause is suspected to have been poison, be careful to tie the stomach at both ends before its removal, and keep it and its contents in cleaned, sealed vessels under your own eye and custody, till a chemical analysis can be made. If a person is dying from violence (poison or wounds), when called to him, inform him of the fact, and if he volunteers a statement of the circumstances causing his injuries, or in regard to his assailants, take his words down at once in his exact language, as such a statement will be received in court as if made under oath, provided the person makes it under the belief that he is about to die of his injuries.

The mottled, reddish or livid patches, and the purplish-black discolorations which appear on bodies shortly after death, occasion a great deal of talk and exaggeration among the laity, and are often cited as evidence of the malignant or putrefactive nature of the death sickness, or as proof of ante-mortem violence—while really due to post-mortem contraction of the walls of the arteries, which squeeze the greater part of their blood into the veins, through whose flaccid coats a portion of its separated coloring matter escapes into the surrounding tissues, creating the appearance mentioned. The escaped fluid tends gradually to collect by the law of gravity in the most dependent parts of the body, as the back of the neck, trunk and limbs, thus leaving the higher parts clear and wax-like in appearance.

You can always distinguish these post-mortem appearances, from bruises inflicted during life, by making an incision into them. If post-mortem, you will find the blood stain superficial and not involving the tissues beneath, but the contrary if due to violence during life. In the latter case, moreover, they cannot be removed by pressure or change in the position of the body.

The popular belief is that if a sudden death begins at the heart there must have been a pre-existing heart disease, and the family physician is often reproached for not having discovered it during the patient's lifetime. Explain that the healthiest heart may suddenly become paralyzed or mechanically occluded and sudden death result. Bear in mind that the ordinary termination of organic heart disease is not sudden, but very slow death, preceded by dropsy, inability to lie down, etc., in fact with the exception of cases of aortic stenosis, or regurgitation, or fatty degeneration, there are few if any forms of organic heart disease that cause sudden death. Of course, syncope, from mental emotion, or physical exhaustion, if not promptly and properly met, may cause sudden death, even when the heart is entirely free from disease.

A belief that stout, healthy people endure accidents, operations, accouchements, diseases, etc., better than weaker, complaining people, is another popular error. The truth is the latter are schooled to pain, to disordered functions, lack of exercise, etc., and when they have to endure afflictions they are not so far from their usual condition as the former, and have not so much strength to be perverted into morbid action, and are in most cases very much more favorable patients. Plethoric systems bear depletion by bloodletting, purgation, etc., badly, because their circulation is accustomed to a certain degree of tension and fulness, anything short of which causes disturbance of the different functions. The loss of a few ounces of blood will sometimes cause a plethoric man to faint, while a thinner one might have lost that quantity without injury.

Old persons seldom bear surgical operations well, especially if they have any disease of the urinary apparatus. Make it a rule *always to* examine the condition of their urine before operating. If any such patients die after you have interfered with their harmless growths or deformities, or with ailments which they have endured for years with only a certain amount of inconvenience, you will probably be strongly censured.

You will seldom be censured for a fatal issue in the diseases of the aged, and never in those of hard drinkers, or in cases where you have given an unfavorable prognosis from the first. On the other hand, if a woman dies in confinement and there is any possible chance to blame you, it will be done, for the reason that bringing forth children is unlike disease. Child-bearing is designed by nature to increase and not to diminish the number of our race; therefore death in labor, which is a physiological function, or during the lying-in, which is a physiological state, seems to be against nature and excites the wonder and criticism of everybody.

Wretched patients who are suffering acutely, perhaps afflicted with painful incurable diseases, and the miserable melancholiacs who are a burden to themselves and to others, will occasionally entreat you to give them something to cause death and put them out of their misery. Likewise, friends of those who are undergoing terrible sufferings from which recovery is impossible, will also sometimes hint at or even openly request that you give the patient a sleeping potion from which he will never awake.

In many such cases you will agree that were God to take the sufferer it would be a blessing; yet with this aspect of the case you have nothing to do. In refusing such solicitations, let your argument be that since a person has no right to end his own existence, he cannot delegate such a right to another, and even if he could, you would be the wrong person to ask, since your province, as a physician, is to prolong life, not to shorten it.

In accidents obscure as to nature or degree, and in cases of sudden illness, when you are pressed to say whether you think the case is dangerous, or likely to be of long duration, choose your language deliberately and give only indefinite answers, until you see whether any new symptoms will develop, whether the system will react, and whether there will be a response to the remedies used. During the progress of such cases be careful to school your features and your manner, that people may not read your hesitations, surprises and uncertainties and either force consultations on you or entirely displace you.

In cases of accident and injury to people found in an insensible condition, although you may strongly suspect this to be due to drunkenness, have the presence of mind to give a *provisional* opinion only, until they return to a sober state. It is better to say, " He is certainly comatose; whether his insensibility is due to alcohol or other causes affecting the brain, it is at this time impossible for any one to say."

It is well when called to cases of burns, cuts, lacerations, fractures, bites, etc., to *mention incidentally* the possibility of erysipelas, pyæmia, lockjaw, etc., and of deformity, or permanent impairment, or whatever other unpleasant results may be reasonably feared, that the parties may know that you are awake to all the possibilities and probabilities of the case. Regarding burns, remember that the gravity of a case is due less to its depth than to the number of square inches involved.

In the course of your professional career you will meet humanity in all its aspects and phases, and your patients will differ greatly in the amount of complaint which they will make in detailing their subjective symptoms to you. Some who are naturally stoical and apathetic will fall into the error of *understating* their true condition, fearing that a fuller statement may alarm their friends, or lead you to think their case serious and prescribe for them much strong medicine, or cause you to pay them many visits. Such patients will sometimes die almost without giving a sign. Others, again, of a hysterical or nervous temperament, fearing that you may not consider them as sick as they really are, will, in detailing their symptoms, *magnify* every detail and seek in every way to impress you and others with an exaggerated idea of the intensity of their sufferings and the gravity of their condition. One of the many advantages which a regular attendant has over other physicians is his familiarity with these peculiarities of temperament, with the extent of the vocabulary each of his patients employs, and with the amount of precision which each uses in answering questions and in describing his sufferings. A fine lady, a hod-carrier, a lawyer and a sailor would each use a different kind of language to express the same symptoms.

In spite of your best endeavors, you will often be criticized, or upbraided for your lack of foresight regarding the recovery or death of patients. The ability to estimate the vital resistance in each case, by the look, visage, voice, attitude, movements and general appearance of the patient, is necessary to the perfection of your skill as a physician. It is something apart from your diagnosis, pathological and therapeutical, and few attain it.

The truth is that life is a *different* quantity in different people, and you will usually have no other way to judge a patient's prospect of recovery, than by the *average* human standard. You will sometimes have cases which will surprise you by their having a great deal *less* than the *average* tenacity of life, and others by having a great deal *more* than the average; and no matter how careful you are, you cannot, with our present knowledge, accurately and unfailingly prognosticate the endurance power of every patient.

To illustrate what is meant:

HEALTH, ... 0.

CLASSES. · · . . . .
{
1st.
2d.
3d.
4th.
5th.
6th.
7th.
}

Suppose the above seven figures to represent the various degrees of mankind's ability to endure sickness and injury, and that the fourth figure represents the average extent of human endurance power: some patients, then, will actually succumb and die like sheep if the first degree is passed, some if the second is touched, others can endure to the third, and so on, while still others have tenacity of life enough to recover after going as low as the fifth, or even the sixth degree. Now, if you could penetrate each patient's vital recesses and gauge the total of *his* endurance power,— could see at what point *his* possibility of recovery ends and *his* dissolution begins, you could solve the great problem of life—there would be fewer unanswerable how's and why's, and you would seldom, if ever, be reproached for unpredicted terminations. This you cannot do, but *you can* in every case make full use of *all* the teachings of experience, *and must* avail yourself of *every aid* offered to you by medical science.

Human nature is the same everywhere. The prince in his palace and the beggar in his hovel, the citizen in his mansion and the felon in his dungeon, the sailor on his ship and the soldier in his tent—all nations and all religions, the Christian, the Jew and the Pagan, all feel the same fears and anxieties, and all turn their eyes and their hearts to the physician when sickness invades or death threatens; because life and health are prized above all things else on earth. This makes the physician's visit the chief event of a sick person's day, and causes each patient anxiously to watch for his approach.

Bear this ever in mind, and wherever your lot is cast, observe punctuality and system in attending those under your care. Also remember always that every phase of

18

your conduct, every word you utter, every look, every shrug of the shoulders, every nod of the head, will be noticed, and may be dwelt upon after you depart.

Thus, my professional brothers, I would attempt to show that the more closely a physician studies the moral and mental infirmities and idiosyncrasies of the various classes who make up the community, the more clearly he will see that the practice of medicine has a peculiar and complex environment, and that he should make skill in preventing, relieving and curing disease, his central thought and chief reliance, and should discharge every duty with fidelity and honor; but, further, that he must also show professional tact and business sagacity, if he would succeed in his profession, create for himself a sphere of usefulness in the world, and do justice to himself and to those dependent upon him.

In conclusion, let me add, that if the suggestions of this little work shall enable you to discern the path of duty with greater clearness, and to follow it with increased hope and determination, or shall teach you to wield your powers with greater success, it will fully accomplish the object of your well-wisher and co-worker.

THE AUTHOR.

INDEX.

INDEX.

281

The publishers have placed on the next two pages a few commendations from well-known sources; also, on the page following them, an advertisement.

EXTRACTS FROM A FEW OF THE MANY LETTERS RECEIVED BY THE AUTHOR.

I have read "The Physician Himself" with pleasure—delight. It is brimful of medical and social philosophy; every doctor in the land can study it with pleasure and profit. I wish I could have read such a work thirty years ago.

PROF. JOHN S. LYNCH,
Baltimore, Md.

"The Physician Himself" interested me so much that I actually read it through at one sitting. It is brimful of the very best advice possible for medical men. I, for one, shall try to profit by it.

PROF. WILLIAM GOODELL,
Philadelphia.

The book has given me great pleasure, and reflects great credit by both its philosophical and practical spirit.

PROF. A. JACOBI,
New York.

I would be glad if in the true interest of the profession in "Old England," some able practitioner here would prepare a work for us on the same line as "The Physician Himself."

DR. JUKES DE STYRAP,
Shrewsbury, England.

It is full of valuable suggestions.

PROF. WM. A. HAMMOND,
New York.

I shall recommend it to the students of the "Quincy College of Medicine" as worth a thousand of the Hippocratic oath. The advice in it should by them be taken, a beacon by day and a guiding star by night.

PROF. WM. A. BYRD,
Quincy, Ill.

It is a valuable production. I have read it with much pleasure and instruction.

PROF. ISAAC E. TAYLOR,
President Medical Faculty of Bellevue College.

It is a marvel of common sense, second only to the Bible in value to any young physician.

DR. CHARLES C. PIKE,
Peabody, Mass.

"The Physician Himself" is replete with sound suggestions. Its perusal would be profitable to all practitioners, and doubly so to the younger ones, whom it will enable to begin right.

PROF. C. A. LINDSLEY,
Dean of Yale College.

I wish every young medical man would commit the thoughts it suggests to memory, for he had better be below mediocrity in physic and learned in practical wisdom, than to be learned in physic and deficient in everyday practical matters.

DR. GEORGE M. BEARD,
New York.

Its suggestions are of interest and use, especially to the young physician.

PROF. A. B. PALMER,
University of Michigan.

This book is evidently the production of an unspoiled mind and the fruit of a ripe career. I admire its pure tone and feel the value of its practical points. How I wish I could have read such a guide at the outset of my career!

PROF. JAMES NEVINS HYDE,
Chicago, Ill.

It is full of good suggestions and admirable advice which will prove very advantageous to our profession.

DR. J. K. BARNES,
Surgeon-General U. S. Army.

It contains a great deal of good sense, well expressed.

PROF. OLIVER WENDELL HOLMES,
Harvard University.

I have just this minute finished reading "The Physician Himself," and cannot treat myself so inhumanly as to resist the temptation to thank you. I have been in practice twenty-four years, and flatter myself that I have been moderately successful, yet from the depths of my heart I thank you for writing this book. On the blank part of page 203 I have written the following:
"I never before got as much for the same amount of money as I did when I bought this book."

DR. RICHARD ANDERSON,
Albemarle, N. C.

Its views on morals and ethics are correct, and its paragraphs on the relations between physicians and pharmacists are equally just and commendable.

PROF. RICHARD McSHERRY,
University of Maryland.

"The Physician Himself" is useful alike to the tyro and the sage—the neophyte and the veteran. It is a headlight in the splendor of whose beams a multitude of our profession shall find their way to success.

PROF. J. M. BODINE,
Dean, University of Louisville.

It is replete with good sense and sound philosophy. No man can read it without realizing that its author is a Christian, a gentleman and a shrewd observer.

PROF. EDWARD WARREN (Bey),
Chevalier of the Legion of Honor, etc., Paris, France.

This book is marvellously full of good suggestions and good sense. The reading of it reminds one of the egg story of Columbus. Every physician can solve the problems that most interest him, now that Dr. Cathell has broken the shell and made it flat-bottomed.

PROF. A. REEVES JACKSON,
Dean Chicago College of Physicians and Surgeons.

It is evidently based upon actual experience and a thorough knowledge of human nature, and discusses various questions with strong common sense.

PROF. I. E. ATKINSON,
University of Maryland.

I have read "The Physician Himself" with great care. It is a most excellent work—full of wisdom, and gives facts that if faithfully followed will lead to renown and professional success.

PROF. A. P. DUTCHER,
Cleveland, O.

I have read "The Physician Himself" carefully. I find it an admirable work, and shall advise our Janitor to keep a stock on hand in the book department of Bellevue.

PROF. WM. T. LUSK,
New York.

"The Physician Himself" certainly contains a great many very excellent suggestions.

PROF. J. M. DACOSTA,
Philadelphia, Pa.

It must impress all its readers with the belief that it was written by an able and honest member of the profession and for the good of the profession.

PROF. W. H. BYFORD,
Chicago, Ill.

Its publication is timely. It contains information calculated to be of great advantage. I do not know where else could be found so many well-digested, well-arranged practical hints.

DR. PHILIP S. WALES,
Surgeon-General U. S. Navy.

EXTRACTS FROM MEDICAL JOURNALS.

It is marked with good common sense, and replete with excellent maxims and suggestions for the guidance of medical men.—*The British Medical Journal*, London.

The book is a mine of practical hints.—*The Archives of Medicine*, New York.

There is scarcely an emergency, in a business point of view, that a man cannot be equal to, if he will follow out strictly the advice of Dr. Cathell. He deserves a vote of thanks from the younger members of the profession.—*The Louisville Medical Herald*.

We strongly advise every actual and intending practitioner of medicine or surgery to have "The Physician Himself," and the more it influences his future conduct the better he will be.—*The Canada Medical and Surgical Journal*, Montreal.

Nothing seems to have been left unsaid, and no point untouched.—*The San Francisco Western Lancet*.

Rarely do we find such a practical combination of good common sense, purity of counsel, and strength of style as in "The Physician Himself." We unhesitatingly recommend it, and are certain all who read it will find most healthy engagement in its perusal.—*The New Orleans Medical and Surgical Journal*.

There is not a subject connected with the personal welfare of the medical man mentally, morally or ethically, left untouched.—*The Chicago Medical Journal and Examiner*.

The advice it contains counsels nothing that would be unbecoming a gentleman and a physician. The physician just starting upon his professional career, let it be in town or country, should by all means read it, and after its perusal he will undoubtedly feel himself under a debt of gratitude to the author.—*The Medical and Surgical Reporter*, Philadelphia.

It is full of pithy suggestions, every one of which is almost axiomatic.—*St. Louis Medical and Surgical Journal*.

The amount of useful, practical information "The Physician Himself" succeeds in conveying to its readers is simply astonishing, and its practical value to the profession can hardly be over-estimated.—*The Medical Herald*, St. Joseph, Missouri.

We can only say, if its teachings are followed it will insure success in the career of any physician.—*The Southern Clinic*, Richmond.

It points out all the stumbling-blocks, and the reader acquires in a few hours that which the elder members of the profession have attained by years of attrition in society.—*The Mississippi Valley Medical Monthly*, Memphis, Tenn.

We would advise every doctor to well weigh the advice given in this book, and govern his conduct accordingly.—*The Virginia Medical Monthly*.

The doctor who starts on his career knowing and practising the ethical and business maxims here recorded, will be saved many a false step, and the doctor who attempts to go on with less will eventually have to pay dearly for his experience.—*The North Carolina Medical Journal*.

The volume is full of practical hints for a beginner, and we would advise all raw recruits in the profession to get it and read it.—*The Pacific Medical and Surgical Reporter*, San Francisco.

"The Physician Himself" is unique and has been received with universal favor for its shrewd, practical common sense.—*Quinan's Medical Annals of Baltimore*.

Of all the books that have been placed before the Medical readers of America, none have attracted such universally favorable comment as the unique little book of Dr. Cathell. That it has gone through three large editions in one year speaks more approvingly than anything that we could possibly say in regard to it. We can conscientiously say, that no one can read it and not be benefited.—*The Southern Practitioner*, Nashville, Tenn.

It is full of valuable suggestions.—*The New York Medical Record*.

Whatever others may think, we feel that there is in this book just that something which we have always lacked—that something which no previous work has supplied. By pointing out the best course in many of the embarrassing situations of professional life, the author has rendered the profession, and especially the younger members of it, a service for which we feel he will in the end be both thanked and compensated. The practical value of the book can hardly be overstated.—*The Maryland Medical Journal*.

Every medical practitioner will find "The Physician Himself" a most valuable book.—*The Sanitarian*, New York.

Prof. Cathell has evidently made a thorough study of the habits and customs of his brother physicians, and has hence produced a book of the most intensely interesting character. Why Dr. A is so very successful; why Dr. B is, with an equal amount of brains, much less so: and why, finally, Dr. C, with more brains than either, has entirely failed in acquiring even a moderate living out of his practice, are all as plain to Prof. C.'s vision as the simplest problem in geometry. It is one of the most valuable books published in the last twenty-five years.—*Baltimore Medical Chronicle*.

Every part bristles with practical facts, acquired only by experience. We believe it contains the key to success.—*The New England Medical Monthly*.

It bristles all over with common sense hints and shrewd observations regarding human nature as the doctor meets it, and shows the importance of professional tact and business sagacity. It touches on the hundred an one different matters that go to make up the successful physician, and will make successful aspirants for fame of those who otherwise, with all their talents, might have wasted their fragrance on the desert air and gained neither reputation nor competence.—*The New York Medical Gazette*.

"The Physician Himself" does what no other work has ever done; it treats of matters which are the keystone of the brilliant success of many practitioners, and the lack of which has ruined the prospects of many a bright career.—*The Missouri Valley Medical Journal*.

The task that the author has undertaken is certainly a commendable, timely, and arduous one, and the manner in which he has accomplished it is as commendable, thorough, honorable, and worldly-wise.—*Archives of Laryngology*, New York City.

The path of duty is clearly indicated in this book, and when followed will be certain to advance the welfare of our honorable profession.—*The International Review of Medical and Surgical Technics*, Boston, Mass.

This volume will repay a careful perusal. Its tone is high. It is written in a spirited style and sets forth clearly and forcibly much good advice for all young men who desire to avoid mistakes of a personal and social kind, but on the principle of "never too late to mend," we believe that old practitioners may derive great many hints from it.—*The Edinburgh* (Scotland) *Medical Journal*.

THE FOURTH EDITION

OF

THE PHYSICIAN HIMSELF

BY D. W. CATHELL, M. D.

Will be sent by mail to any address upon receipt of $2.00,
by the publishers,

CUSHINGS & BAILEY,

262 WEST BALTIMORE STREET,

BALTIMORE, MD.

VHO KEEP CONSTANTLY ON HAND A FULL AND COMPLETE STOCK OF

MEDICAL BOOKS.

CATALOGUE OF MEDICAL WORKS FURNISHED ON APPLICATION.

ALSO KEEP ON HAND A COMPLETE STOCK OF

CLASSICAL, LAW AND MISCELLANEOUS BOOKS,

AND

FOREIGN AND DOMESTIC STATIONERY,

Which they offer for Sale at Low Prices.